Can You Believe It?

Stories and Idioms from Real Life

D1567493

Oxford University Press
198 Madison Avenue
New York, NY 10016 USA

Great Clarendon Street
Oxford OX2 6DP England

Oxford New York

*Athens Auckland Bangkok Bogota Buenos Aires
Calcutta Cape Town Chennai Dar es Salaam
Delhi Florence Hong Kong Istanbul Karachi
Kuala Lumpur Madrid Melbourne Mexico City
Mumbai Nairobi Paris São Paulo Singapore
Taipei Tokyo Toronto Warsaw*

and associated companies in
Berlin Ibadan

OXFORD is a trademark of Oxford University Press.

ISBN 0-19-437275-8

Library of Congress Cataloging-In-Publication Data
Huizenga, Jann
     Stories and idioms from real life / Jann Huizenga.
          p. cm. -- (Can you believe it?)
     Includes index.
     ISBN 0-19-437275-8
          1. English language--Textbooks for foreign
speakers. 2.
     English language--Idioms--Problems, exercises, etc. 3.
Readers--
     Manners and customs. I.Title. II. Series
PE1128.H7845 1999
428.2"4--dc21   99-042-79

Editorial Manager: Susan Lanzano
Editor: Lynne Barsky
Senior Production Editor: Robyn F. Clemente
Design Manager: Lynne Torrey
Designer: Brett Sonnenschein
Senior Art Buyer: Patricia Marx
Photo Researcher: Laura Nash
Production Manager: Abram Hall
Production Coordinator: Shanta Persaud

Printing (last digit): 10 9 8 7 6 5 4 3 2 1

Printed in the United States.

Acknowledgments

Illustrations by Carlos Castellanos, Patrick Merrell, Wally Neibart,
Lori Oseiki, William Waitzman

Realia by Maj Hagsted, Rita Lascaro

Cover illustration by Ken Condon

*The publishers would like to thank the following for their permission
to reproduce photographs:* Adam Basma/Adam Basma Dance Co.; Jim
Tuten/Animals, Animals; Gerard Lacz/Peter Arnold; Dennis Doyle/AP;
Comstock; Jean-Marc Giboux/Gamma Liaison; Barros & Barros,
Frank Whitney/Image Bank; Peter Marlow/Magnum; James
Wardell/Masterfile; Janis Christie, Don Farrall, C. Lee (Photolink),
Doug Meneuz, S. Pearce (Photolink)/Photodisc; Robert Pisano/REI;
Tassanee Vejpongsa/Reuters (Archive photo); Tony Stone; Superstock;
Mark M. Lawrence, Chuck Savage, Mark Tuschman/The Stock Market

Credits

The stories in this book have been adapted from the following material:
p. 2, National Public Radio's Morning Edition, January 27, 1998; **p.** 5,
The San Diego Union-Tribune, February 1, 1998; **p.** 6, National Public
Radio's Morning Edition, 1998; **p.** 10, Reader's Digest; **p.** 13, The New
Mexican (from the Associated Press), November 22, 1997; **p.** 14, The
New Yorker, October 20 and 27, 1997; **p.** 18, The New Mexican (from
the Associated Press) November 22, 1997; **p.** 26, The New York Times,
December 28, 1997; **p.** 29, The New Mexican (from the Associated
Press), December 25, 1997; **p.** 30, The New Mexican, August 29, 1996;
p. 34, The New Mexican, October 12, 1997; **p.** 38, The New Mexican,
January 12, 1996; **p.** 42, The San Diego Union Tribune, January 1,
1998; **p.** 50, The Associated Press on-line, March 26, 1998; **p.** 54, The
New Mexican, February 18, 1998; **p.** 58, The New Mexican; **p.** 62, The
New York Times, November 2, 1997; **p.** 65, The Associated Press on-
line, 1998; **p.** 66, The New York Times, February 28, 1998; **p.** 74, The
Associated Press on-line, December 19, 1998; **p.** 78, People, September
2, 1996; **p.** 81, The New Mexican, October 17, 1995; **p.** 82, News reports
and personal communication from Disney World spokespeople; **p.** 86,
The New Mexican (from the Associated Press), June 11, 1993; **p.** 89,
The New Mexican (from the Associated Press), October 22, 1997; **p.** 90,
Prime Time Live (TV), November 12, 1997.

Can You Believe It?

Stories and Idioms from Real Life

Book 2

Jann Huizenga

OXFORD
UNIVERSITY PRESS

To the Student

In this book you will enjoy learning everyday idiomatic American English through amazing, true stories from around the world.

When you study vocabulary, it is not enough to learn individual words. Everyday English is filled with expressions that are two or more words long, such as *keep on, give someone the green light,* and *after a while.* These expressions are essential to successful communication in English, and they need to be learned as individual units, in the same way as individual words. In this book you will find **idioms, fixed expressions,** and **phrasal verbs**.

What is an idiom?

An **idiom** is a group of words that has a meaning different from the meaning of its individual parts. In the example below, you probably know all the individual words, but you still may not understand the meaning of the expression. This is because the expressions are idiomatic.

My family feels blue about my trip, but I am on top of the world.

Feel blue means *feel sad; be on top of the world* means *feel very happy.*

What is a fixed expression?

Be interested in, be in a hurry, and *make a mistake* are **fixed expressions**. You will understand the whole expression if you know the meaning of the parts. But the translation of a fixed expression into your language may not be word for word.

What is a phrasal verb?

A **phrasal verb** is a verb followed by a particle such as *in, at, on, for,* etc. *Look for* and *look after* are phrasal verbs that mean *try to find* and *take care of.* Phrasal verbs are usually idiomatic. You can learn more about phrasal verbs in Appendix D, page 114.

The steps to learning idioms in this book are as follows:
1. **Read** the story quickly to get the main idea.
2. **Listen** several times to the story while you look at pictures to get used to the idioms.
3. **Read** the story again and study the idioms.
4. **Tell** the story using the idioms while looking only at pictures.
5. **Talk** about the story and then about yourself using the idioms.
6. **Write** about yourself using the idioms.
7. **Take a dictation** that uses the idioms.
8. **Fill in the blanks** in a dialogue or story using the idioms. Then **role-play** the dialogue or tell the story.

Extra study aids to use with this textbook include:

- A listening cassette

- **Appendix A:** An Answer Key (page 98)

- **Appendix B:** Dictations (page 102)

- **Appendix C:** An appendix that groups the idioms in the book in various ways to help you remember their form and meaning (page 105)

- **Appendix D:** An appendix that explains the grammar of phrasal verbs (page 112) and gives a list of phrasal verbs (page 113)

- **Lexicon:** A list of all the idioms (with definitions) in the book, that gives further examples, language notes, and idiomatic synonyms and antonyms (page 116)

To the Teacher

A general introduction

The goal of *Can You Believe It? Book 2* is to teach high-frequency idioms, two-word verbs, and fixed expressions in the context of true, memorable stories to ESL/EFL students at a high-beginning level. It is founded on two basic premises: 1) that everyone loves a good story, and 2) that vocabulary acquisition occurs more readily when new items are embedded in engaging, whole contexts and used in tasks that have meaning and purpose. The book is written for classroom use, but it will also work well for self-study when used with the audio program.

Thanks in part to Michael Lewis's influential work on lexical issues, TESOL professionals are increasingly aware that idioms and fixed expressions form a significant part of the lexicon of English and are central to natural language use. These prefabricated multi-word expressions must be acquired as wholes in the same way as individual words. *Can You Believe It?* teaches the following kinds of high-frequency fixed lexical expressions:

- traditional, graphic idioms, such as: *give someone the green light, cost an arm and a leg;*
- non-traditional idioms, such as: *spend time, throw a party, change one's mind;*
- two- or three-word adverbial chunks, such as: *now and then, right away, all at once;*
- two- or three-word phrasal verbs, such as: *give up, be interested in, get rid of;* and,
- common expressions consisting of de-lexicalized verbs, such as: *make* or *get* plus a noun or adjective (*get lost, make money*), word partnerships that are likely to produce translation mistakes and need to be learned as chunks.

Can You Believe It? is compatible with comprehension approaches such as The Natural Approach. The picture sequences that correspond to the stories provide the basis for great "comprehensible input," so the book can be used for listening comprehension and general language acquisition at beginning levels as well as for the specific mastery of idioms and expressions.

The approach thoroughly integrates the four skills of listening, reading, speaking, and writing. Activities are sequenced so that input precedes output. The initial approach relies heavily on listening, with picture sequences used as visual supports for comprehension. It is through this richly contextualized (and repeated) listening that students begin to make hypotheses about the new expressions and develop a feel for their use. Students then go on to read the story—an essential step that will provide welcome written reinforcement for visually oriented learners and will help all students with their literacy skills. After students' pumps have been primed, so to speak, with the listening and reading input, they are ready to begin producing the idioms in speaking and writing. The output activities become progressively more demanding; these include story retelling, thought-provoking personal questions, dialogue production, and dictation.

Researchers contend that we acquire new lexical items by meeting them a number of times (seven times, some say). Thus, in *Can You Believe It?*, students will revisit the idioms and expressions many times within each unit as well as in review units and, to some extent, from unit to unit. (The idioms that are recycled between units have been indicated as such in the Table of Contents, as well as in the New Idioms and Expressions Box which follows the reading.)

Extra Features

Listening Cassette
The cassette features dramatic readings of all the stories in the text and dictations for each unit (from **Appendix B**). The stories are read by different actors with varying voices and styles so students are exposed to language variety.

Answer Key (Appendix A)
Students who use the book independently will especially appreciate this feature, though classroom teachers will also find it handy.

Idiom Groups (Appendix C)

This appendix is a rich resource for those students who would like a better sense of how the idioms in *Can You Believe It?* can be grouped together semantically.

Phrasal Verbs (Appendix D)

Simple but detailed grammar explanations of phrasal verbs are included here for students who feel ready for this information.

Lexicon

The Lexicon gives extra information about each idiom and fixed expression in the book. Definitions, additional examples, grammar information, more collocations, and idiomatic synonyms and antonyms are included.

Specific Teaching Suggestions

The exercises and activities in each unit can be used in a variety of ways, and you are encouraged to experiment and adapt them as you see fit. The suggested sequence can be changed, depending on your goals and your specific class needs. Below are some suggestions for classroom use.

1. Quick Reading

Before students read the story quickly to get the gist, have them do one of the following prediction activities:

   a. Cover the story and look at the picture sequence on the opposite page. Discuss (in pairs or small groups) what the story seems to be about.

   b. Cover the story. Look at the title and the picture on the story page. Make predictions about the story.

Then ask students to read the story quickly just to get the main idea or the basic story line. You might give them a time limit of two or three minutes for this. (The details of the story will become clear during Exercise 2 as they listen to it repeatedly while looking at the picture sequence.) Previewing the story in this manner will allow students, especially those who are stronger visual than oral/aural learners, to relax and better comprehend the story and the new idioms in context during the listening "input" stage. It is best to have students read silently at this stage since they will want to process the text in their own ways.

2. Listen

Ask students to cover the story. Play the cassette or, if you prefer, read the story to students. If you are not using the cassette, be sure to say the numbers as you move from picture to picture so students can follow (at least during the first listening). Tell the story at a natural speed, pausing somewhat longer than usual at the end of breath groups and sentences. This will give students important processing time. The goal of this activity is to provide students with truly "comprehensible input," i.e., an acquisition stage in which a high degree of contextualization will allow them to formulate hypotheses and discover meaning in language that they are hearing for the first time. Making inferences and hypotheses about new language in context is a skill that all language learners need to feel comfortable with; this exercise thus develops good learning strategies while helping students acquire new language. During a second or third telling of the story, you may want to write the new idioms on the board, as reinforcement for your visually oriented students. (The easiest thing would be to write them on the board prior to the retelling and point to them as they occur.)

As an assessment technique (to see how well students have understood and internalized the new expressions in the story), tell students you are going to talk about the pictures out of order. They should point to the picture you are describing. Or, as an alternative, retell the story making some major "mistakes." Have students signal somehow (by raising their hands, making faces, or making a buzzing sound) when they hear a mistake.

3. Read the Story

Your more visual learners will be especially eager to take a closer look at the story at this point, double-checking their hypotheses with the New Idioms and Expressions box. After students have had some silent time for re-reading, you might want to have them read aloud for pronunciation practice. Volunteers could take turns reading to the whole class, or pairs could read to each other, helping each other with pronunciation. You may want to do part or all of Exercise 6 at this point (see suggestions below).

For a bit of extra practice with the idioms, and as a good lead-in to Exercise 4, you could conduct the following matching activity: Write the unit idioms on slips of paper or index cards. Cut the idioms in half. Give half to each student. Tell students to stand up, walk around the room, and find the other halves of their idioms. As a check, have the pairs say their idioms aloud to the whole class.

4. Listen and Complete

This activity functions as a type of assessment, a first step in seeing if students can produce the idioms that they've heard so many times. Play the cassette, or if you prefer, read the story to students, pausing in the middle of expressions. When students hear a pause, they can: 1) freely shout the rest of the idiom or sentence, 2) raise their hands if they know how to complete it and be called on individually, or 3) discuss how to complete the idiom or sentence in pairs or groups before volunteering their answers.

5. Tell the Story

At this point, the exercises move away from recognition into production. Elicit the story orally from the whole class first. Encourage students to call out the ideas of the story in chronological order. They can, of course, look at the picture sequence during this activity, but the story should be covered. The retelling will be a paraphrase of the original story, but students will probably reuse most of the new idioms. (You could have the idioms listed on the board to give students a bit of extra help.) You may want to run this activity as a variation on *Language Experience*, writing down sentences and phrases on the board as students suggest them. Underlining the idioms and fixed expressions that students generate will help to highlight them.

Next, ask students to work in pairs or small groups to retell the story to each other. Once again, make sure they cover the story. One way for them to work is with *Talking Chips*, communication regulators used in *Cooperative Learning*. Working in pairs or groups of three, each student takes four or five *Talking Chips* (e.g., tokens, such as buttons, poker chips, or paint chips). Together, they reconstruct the story. As each student contributes a sentence, he or she puts in a token. (The chips ensure that each student speaks and that all have an equal opportunity to participate.)

6. Answer the Questions

As an alternative to the traditional Whole-Class-Question-Answer here, you might want to try using *Numbered Heads Together*, a *Cooperative Learning* structure. The steps to *Numbered Heads Together* are as follows:

a. Students get into teams of four and number off from 1 to 4.

b. The teacher asks a question.

c. Students on each team literally put their heads together and reach a consensus on the answer and the phrasing of the answer.

d. The teacher calls a number at random. Students with that number raise their hands (or stand up) and report on their team's answer. You will probably want to get each team's answer, as there will be variations to discuss and comment on.

The advantages of this questioning technique over the traditional Whole-Class-Question-Answer are the following: All students are involved since no one knows who will be called on; stronger students help weaker ones; students have "think time" and "rehearsal time" in small groups before they have to respond in front of the whole class; and a wrong response is not so embarrassing because it comes from a team rather than an individual.

The "About you" questions can be answered orally, either in a whole-class setting or in small groups. These questions are also good springboards for paragraph writing. Allow students to choose their favorite ones to respond to, and to share their writing with partners.

7. Write About Yourself

These sentence completions may be somewhat personal, so students may prefer to share them in small groups rather than with the whole class. You might ask volunteers, though, to put their sentences on the board after groups have shared. Be sure that the volunteers understand that correction may be involved!

8. Write a Dialogue

This exercise generally asks students to write short dialogues in pairs, using at least three idioms. Give students time in pairs not only to create the dialogues, but also to rehearse them (and, ideally, to memorize them). Depending on the time you can devote to this activity, you may want to have pairs perform for other pairs and then for the whole class; or you may prefer simply to call on a few volunteers to perform for class. If you can keep a small stash of props (hats, scarves, sunglasses, and other odd items) available for this activity and ask students to use some props as well as appropriate body language as they perform, this task will be greatly enlivened.

9. Take a Dictation

Play the cassette or use **Appendix B** to read students the dictation. A recommended procedure for the dictation is as follows:

a. Read the dictation once at normal speed. Students should not write at this stage.

b. Read the dictation again, this time pausing long enough after each breath group for students to write. (Be sure, in advance, that students know the words *comma* and *period*.)

c. Read the dictation a third time, at near-normal speed, allowing students to check their writing.

Students can correct their own work or the work of a partner using **Appendix B**. Students might also like to try peer dictations, where one student dictates to another.

10. Complete the Dialogue/Story

After students work individually, in pairs, or in groups to fill in the blanks with the idioms and expressions from the box, they can check their answers in **Appendix A**.

Thirteen of the twenty units have a dialogue exercise. Students can practice the dialogue in pairs, perhaps preparing for an expressive reading of the dialogue for the whole class.

The remaining seven units have a story exercise. After filling in the blanks, students can either practice reading the story to each other in pairs or paraphrase it to each other, being sure to use the idioms from the box in the retelling.

Acknowledgments

Many people contributed to *Can You Believe It?*, and I'm grateful to them all. Susan Lanzano at Oxford University Press was the guiding light from start to finish. Lynne Barsky was a generous and patient editor whose care and expertise made this a much better book. Special thanks to Robyn Clemente, production editor, and to the Design team including Lynne Torrey, Brett Sonnenschein, Trish Marx, and Laura Nash. Good friend and colleague Ken Sheppard was crucial in getting the project off the ground, contributing key ideas during an autumnal stroll down Fifth Avenue. Linda Huizenga's help with writing made the project fun, and husband Kim Crowley's constant search for stories yielded some of the best ones. Thanks also to Joel and Dolly for feeding me stories from their local papers. My reviewers were a goldmine of wonderful suggestions and comments:

Lubie Alatriste, New York, NY

Christel Antonellis, Boston, MA

Vicki Blaho, Los Angeles, CA

Susan Burke, Atlanta, GA

Gloria Horton, Pasadena, CA

Tay Lesley, Los Angeles, CA

Ellen Pentkowski, Chicago, IL

Barbara Jane Pers, Brooklyn, NY

Barbara Smith-Palinkas, Tampa, FL

Stephanie Snider, Suffolk County, NY

Candice Ramirez, Moreno Valley, CA

Christine Tierney, Houston, TX

Barbara Webster, Phoenix, AZ

Table of Contents

It's No Wonder!

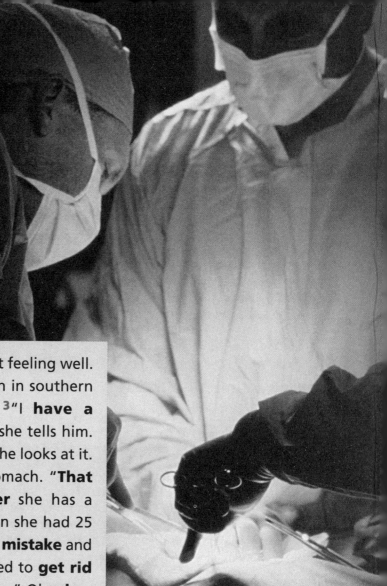

1. Quick Reading

Look at the pictures on page 3.
What is the story about?

Now read quickly to get the main idea.

SARATOV, RUSSIA **¹**One day, Olga Petrovic isn't feeling well. **²**She goes to see the doctor in her small town in southern Russia. **"What's the matter?"** he asks. **³**"I **have a stomachache**. **⁴**And I'm **running a fever**," she tells him. **⁵**The doctor takes an x-ray. He's shocked when he looks at it. There's a 12-inch piece of metal in Olga's stomach. **"That takes the cake!"** he thinks. **"No wonder** she has a stomachache!" **⁶**Olga remembers an operation she had 25 years ago. Apparently, the surgeon **made a** big **mistake** and left a medical instrument inside her. **⁷**"We need to **get rid of** it," says the doctor. "You need an operation." Olga **has cold feet** and wants to **put** it **off**. But her doctor wants her to have the operation **right away**. **⁸**Now the medical instrument is gone and Olga is recovering.

New idioms and expressions

(it's) no wonder	it's not surprising
What's the matter?	What's wrong?
have a stomachache	feel pain in one's stomach
run a fever	have a high body temperature
That takes the cake!	That's really strange!; That's the worst!
make a mistake	do something incorrectly
get rid of something*	remove something
have cold feet	be afraid to do something
put something off*	delay or postpone something
right away	immediately

Words in parentheses ( ) can occur with the idiom, but don't have to.   *phrasal verb (see Lexicon, pp. 116–150 and Appendix D, pp. 112–115)

2. Listen

Cover the story and look only at these pictures. Listen to the story two or three times.

Note: As the tape or your teacher says a number, look at the corresponding picture.

3. Read the Story

Now read the story carefully. Pay special attention to the idioms so that you're ready for Exercise 4.

4. Listen and Complete

Close your book. Listen to the story again. When the tape or your teacher pauses, try to complete the idiom.

5. Tell the Story

Cover the story and look at the pictures above. Tell the story using as many idioms as you can.

a. First, work with the whole class to retell the story.

b. Then tell the story to a partner or small group.

6. Answer the Questions

About the story..

a. What's the matter with Olga when she goes to the doctor?

b. What does the doctor say when he sees the x-ray?

c. What happened to her 25 years ago?

d. Why does Olga need another operation?

e. Why does she want to put it off?

About you..

f. Have you ever had an operation?

g. How do you feel today? Do you have a stomachache, a headache, or a cold?

h. How often do you think doctors make serious mistakes? Tell about a time when *you* made a big mistake.

i. Are you putting off something that you should be doing? If so, what?

j. Is there something you won't do because you have cold feet?

k. Do you have any bad habits that you'd like to get rid of?

7. Write About Yourself

Complete the sentences, writing something true about yourself.

a. When I'm running a fever, I _____.

b. I often put off _____ because

_____.

c. I need to _____ right away.

d. I want to get rid of some of my possessions, including _____

_____.

8. Write a Dialogue

Work with a partner. Write a dialogue using at least three idioms from the unit. Act it out for a small group or the class.

9. Take a Dictation

_____

_____

_____

_____

_____

10. Complete the Story

a. Read this true story and fill in the blanks with idioms from the box.

- it's no wonder
- made the mistake
- get rid of
- is running a fever
- has a stomachache
- right away

Doctors Make a BIG Mistake

San Francisco, CA, USA One day, Richard Kearney, 47, has an operation on his bladder. When he returns home from the hospital, he (1) _has a stomachache_. Several days later, he has a lot of pain and (2) _____.

An X ray shows that there is something large in his stomach. Doctors operate (3) _____ because they know they need to (4) _____ it. When they cut Kearney open, they pull a 2-foot-long towel out of his stomach! Apparently, doctors left it inside him during the first operation.

(5) _____ that Kearney was in pain. He is taking the doctors who (6) _____ to court.

b. Read or tell the story to a partner.

It's About Time! 2

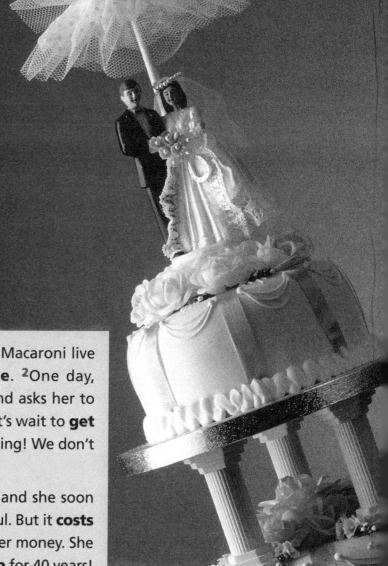

1. Quick Reading

Look at the pictures on page 7.
What is the story about?

Now read quickly to get the main idea.

ANTILLO, ITALY **¹**Vittoria Celemi and Sebastio Macaroni live in a small village in Sicily. They **are in love**. **²**One day, Sebastio gives Vittoria an engagement ring and asks her to marry him. **³**Vittoria accepts, but she adds, "Let's wait to **get married** until we **can afford** the perfect wedding! We don't have enough money now."

⁴Vittoria begins to shop for a wedding dress, and she soon finds the perfect one. It's long, lacy, and beautiful. But it **costs an arm and a leg**! **⁵**So Vittoria starts to save her money. She makes a small payment every year. She **saves up** for 40 years!

⁶At long last, after a 40-year engagement, Vittoria can buy the wedding dress. She and Sebastio decide to **tie the knot**. **⁷**At the wedding, Vittoria looks beautiful in her dress. The newlyweds **are in seventh heaven**. They dance, drink champagne, and eat caviar. **⁸**Afterward, they ride off in a horse-drawn carriage. Their friends watch them and think, **"It's about time!"**

New idioms and expressions

It's about time!	It's later than expected!
be in love (with someone)	love (someone) strongly in a romantic way
get married (to someone)	marry (someone)
can afford something	have enough money to buy something
cost an arm and a leg	be very expensive
save up*	keep money so one can use it later
at long last	after a very long time; finally
tie the knot	marry
be in seventh heaven	be very happy

*phrasal verb (see Lexicon and Appendix D)

2. Listen

Cover the story and look only at these pictures. Listen to the story two or three times.

3. Read the Story

Now read the story carefully. Pay special attention to the idioms so that you're ready for Exercise 4.

4. Listen and Complete

Close your book. Listen to the story again. When the tape or your teacher pauses, try to complete the idiom.

5. Tell the Story

Cover the story and look at the pictures above. Tell the story using as many idioms as you can.

a. First, work with the whole class to retell the story.

b. Then tell the story to a partner or small group.

6. Answer the Questions

About the story..

a. What does Vittoria say to Sebastio when he asks her to marry him?

b. What do you think of Vittoria's decision?

c. How long does it take for the couple to tie the knot?

d. How do the newlyweds feel?

About you...

e. Are you patient? Can you imagine waiting 40 years for anything? If so, what?

f. Take a survey of your classmates. How many are single? How many want to get married? Find out their reasons.

g. Is it important to be in love when you get married? Explain your ideas.

h. In your country, when a man wants to marry a woman, does he need to get permission from her parents? Does he give something to the woman or her family? Does the woman give something to the man or his family?

i. Vittoria's wedding dress cost an arm and a leg. Have you ever bought something that cost an arm and a leg? If so, what?

7. Write About Yourself

Complete the sentences, writing something true about yourself.

a. I'm in seventh heaven when _____

_____.

b. Recently, I bought _____, and it/they cost an arm and a leg.

c. I'm saving up to buy _____ because I can't afford it/them now.

8. Write a Dialogue

Work with a partner. Write a dialogue using at least three idioms from the unit. Act it out for a small group or the class.

9. Take a Dictation

_____

_____

_____

_____

_____

10. Complete the Dialogue

a. Two friends, Eva and Stephanie, are talking. Fill in the blanks with idioms from the box.

- **I'm in seventh heaven**
- **can afford**
- **cost an arm and a leg**
- **get married**
- **tie the knot**
- **it's about time**

Eva, hi! What's new?

Oh, hi, Stephanie. **Guess what!*** Mario and I are going to (1)_____*get married*_____ in June!

Congratulations, (2)___It's abou_____! You've been engaged for five years! I wasn't sure you were ever going to (3)___tie the knot_____.

Yeah. I had cold feet.

But now you're ready?

Yeah, I know Mario's the one for me. (4)_____!

Are you going to have a big wedding?

We don't know yet. I hope so. If we (5)_____ it, I'd like about 300 guests, a dance band, champagne…

Cool. I know a great band—the Hot Peppers. And they don't (6)_____.

Oh, really? I want to get the details, but I should go now. I'll call you soon.

*Guess what!: a way of starting a conversation (informal)

**cool: great (informal)

recycled idiom: have cold feet

b. Work with a partner. Role-play the dialogue together.

A Heart of Gold

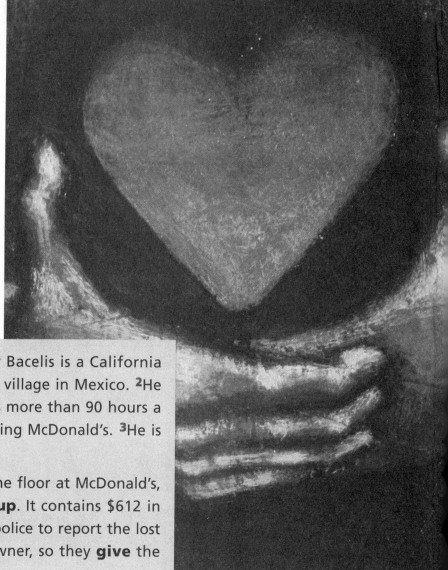

1. Quick Reading

Look at the pictures on page 11.
What is the story about?

Now read quickly to get the main idea.

ORANGE COUNTY, CA, USA ¹Victor Bacelis is a California immigrant who **grew up** in a poor village in Mexico. ²He **is used to** working hard. He works more than 90 hours a week at three different jobs, including McDonald's. ³He is saving up to buy a house.

⁴One day, while Victor is cleaning the floor at McDonald's, he finds an envelope and **picks** it **up**. It contains $612 in cash! ⁵He **gets in touch with** the police to report the lost money. The police can't find the owner, so they **give** the money **back** to Victor.

⁶Then Victor reads a story in the newspaper about Adrian Sandoval, a baby who **is** very **sick**. ⁷Victor decides to **give** the cash **away** to help pay for the baby's surgery. "Life has been nice to me," Bacelis said. "I'**m healthy**. I have enough money. Adrian is a little boy, and his condition really touched me. This is what I want to do." ⁸Victor Bacelis truly **has a heart of gold**.

New idioms and expressions

have a heart of gold · · · · · · · · · · · · · · · · · · ·	have a kind and generous character
grow up* ·	become an adult
be used to (doing) something · · · · · · · ·	be familiar with (doing) something
pick something up* · · · · · · · · · · · · · · · ·	take or lift something off the floor (or a table, etc.)
get in touch with someone · · · · · · · · · ·	contact someone by phone, fax, e-mail, etc.
give something back* · · · · · · · · · · · · ·	return something (to someone)
be sick ·	be unwell; have bad health
give something away* · · · · · · · · · · · · ·	give something as a gift
be healthy ·	be well; have good health

recycled idiom: save up   *phrasal verb (see Lexicon and Appendix D)

2. Listen

Cover the story and look only at these pictures. Listen to the story two or three times.

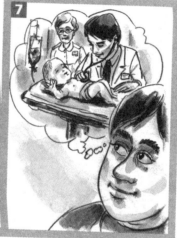

3. Read the Story

Now read the story carefully. Pay special attention to the idioms so that you're ready for Exercise 4.

4. Listen and Complete

Close your book. Listen to the story again. When the tape or your teacher pauses, try to complete the idiom.

5. Tell the Story

Cover the story and look at the pictures above. Tell the story using as many idioms as you can.

a. First, work with the whole class to retell the story.

b. Then tell the story to a partner or small group.

Unit 3   Can You Believe It? **11**

6. Answer the Questions

a. How much money does Victor pick up from the floor?

b. Who does Victor get in touch with?

c. What does he finally do with the cash?

d. What do you know about Victor's past and present life? What kind of man is he?

e. Do you know anyone who has a heart of gold? How does this person act?

f. If you found cash on the floor at work, what would you do? Would you keep the money, get in touch with the police or your boss, or give it away?

g. Are you used to working hard? Tell about your weekly schedule.

h. How do you usually get in touch with friends and family who live far away: by phone, by e-mail, by letter, or by fax?

7. Write About Yourself

Complete the sentences, writing something true about yourself.

a. I grew up in ————————————————.

b. I often get in touch with ————————————————.

c. I'm used to ————————————————.

8. Write a Poem

Write a poem about Victor using at least three idioms from the unit.

Example:

> Victor,
> You **grew up** so poor
> And now you work so hard.
> But still, you **give away** your money.
> You **have a heart of gold**,
> Victor.

9. Take a Dictation

_____

_____

_____

_____

_____

10. Complete the Story

a. Read this true story and fill in the blanks with idioms from the box.

> - is used to
> - gave away
> - was sick
> - are getting in touch with
> - grew up
> - has a heart of gold

Woman Gives Away $11.8 Million

Somerville, New Jersey, USA Eleanor Boyer is a 73-year-old woman who lives alone in a small house in New Jersey, where she (1)_____. She drives an old 1968 Chevrolet.

Eleanor (2)_____ helping other people. She teaches classes at her church. When her mother (3)_____, Eleanor **took care of*** her for seven years. A neighbor says, "Eleanor is the one who shovels everyone's sidewalk when it snows. She (4)_____."

Recently, Eleanor won $11.8 million in the New Jersey State Lottery. What do you think she did with the money? She (5)_____ the entire amount to her church and her town. Now many reporters (6)_____ Eleanor. They are surprised by her actions, but Eleanor seems bored by their questions. "God takes care of me," she declares.

*take care of someone: provide for the needs of someone

b. Read or tell the story to a partner.

Fit as a Fiddle

1. Quick Reading

Look at the pictures on page 15.
What is the story about?

Now read quickly to get the main idea.

BOSTON, MA, USA ¹Ed Rosenthal lives in a nursing home in Boston with other elderly people. ²Ed is a **senior citizen**, 91 years old.

³When Ed was 84 years old, a doctor came to the nursing home. She saw that Ed was **out of shape** and his body was weak. She told him to exercise and get **in shape**. ⁴So Ed started going to the exercise center to **pump iron**. ⁵He **worked out** for seven years, **day in and day out**.

⁶Now Ed has big muscles, and his stomach is **as flat as a pancake**. ⁷He **feels like a million dollars.** ⁸His family and friends are surprised. They can **not believe their eyes**. Now Ed Rosenthal, at 91, is **as fit as a fiddle**!

New idioms and expressions

(as) fit as a fiddle · healthy and physically fit
senior citizen · a person more than 65 years old
out of shape · not in good physical condition
in shape · in good physical condition
pump iron · lift weights
work out* · exercise
day in and day out · regularly; all the time
(as) flat as a pancake · · · · · · · · · · · · · · · · · · very flat
feel like a million dollars · · · · · · · · · · · · · · · be very healthy and happy
not believe one's eyes · · · · · · · · · · · · · · · · · not believe what one sees because of surprise

*phrasal verb (see Lexicon and Appendix D)

2. Listen

Cover the story and look only at these pictures. Listen to the story two or three times.

3. Read the Story

Now read the story carefully. Pay special attention to the idioms so that you're ready for Exercise 4.

4. Listen and Complete

Close your book. Listen to the story again. When the tape or your teacher pauses, try to complete the idiom.

5. Tell the Story

Cover the story and look at the pictures above. Tell the story using as many idioms as you can.

a. First, work with the whole class to retell the story.

b. Then tell the story to a partner or small group.

6. Answer the Questions

About the story...

a. Describe Ed seven years ago. How is he different now?

b. How did he get in shape?

c. What do Ed's friends think of the change?

d. What is a nursing home? Do you think senior citizens like Ed should live in nursing homes?

About you..

e. Do you work out? If so, how often? Where? What do you do? Do you pump iron?

f. What things do you do day in and day out?

g. When you're Ed's age, what kind of shape will you be in?

7. Write About Yourself

Complete the sentences, writing something true about yourself.

a. In my opinion, the best ways to stay as fit as a fiddle are _____

_____.

b. When I'm a senior citizen, _____

_____.

c. I feel like a million dollars when _____

_____.

8. Write a Dialogue

Work with a partner. Write a dialogue using at least three idioms from the unit. Act it out for a small group or the class.

9. Take a Dictation

_____

_____

_____

_____

_____

10. Complete the Dialogue

a. A young girl, Ana, is talking to her grandfather. Fill in the blanks with idioms from the box.

> - in shape
> - out of shape
> - senior citizen
> - fit as a fiddle
> - not believe her eyes
> - feel like a million dollars
> - work out

Grandpa, do you want to go for a bike ride with me today?

No, I don't think so.

Come on,* Grandpa! Please!

Give me a break,** Ana. I'm a (1)_____, you know. I'm much too (2)_____ to ride a bike.

You should (3)_____ like Grandma. She's as (4)_____!

All right, all right. I know I should get (5)_____. I'll go with you if we don't go too far or too fast.

Oh, thanks, Grandpa! We'll just ride to the park. You're going to (6)_____ after you exercise.

Your grandmother will (7)_____ when she sees me on a bike!

* Come on!: Please do it! (informal)

** give someone a break: stop bothering someone (informal)

b. Work with a partner. Role-play the dialogue together.

The Longest Hair in the World

5

1. Quick Reading

Look at the pictures on page 19.
What is the story about?

Now read quickly to get the main idea.

MON NGA, THAILAND ¹Eighty-five-year-old Hoo Sateow lives in a small village in Thailand. ²He has very long hair. **In fact**, it's the longest hair in the world—more than 17 feet long! ³"I cut my hair when I was 18 years old, and I **got sick**. So I'll never do it again," Hoo says. ⁴**According to** Hoo, his long hair allows him to talk to ghosts and help sick people. ⁵Hoo **has something in common with** his older brother, Yi. Both have very long hair. Yi's hair is more than 14 feet long.

⁶Hoo washes his hair only **once in a blue moon**. His friends usually **give him a hand**. ⁷The long hair **takes ages** to dry. Hoo hangs it on a fence in the sun. ⁸His hair is hard to **take care of**, but Hoo says it **comes in handy** in Thailand's cool mountain weather. "I wrap my hair around my head and then **put** my hat **on**. It keeps me warm."

New idioms and expressions

in fact	really, actually
get sick	become unwell or unhealthy
according to someone or something	as someone or something says
have something in common with someone	be similar to another person in some way
once in a blue moon	very rarely
give someone a hand	help someone
take ages	take a very long time
take care of someone or something*	provide for the needs of someone or something
come in handy	be useful or convenient
put something on*	dress in something; place something on oneself

*phrasal verb (see Lexicon and Appendix D)

2. Listen

Cover the story and look only at these pictures. Listen to the story two or three times.

3. Read the Story

Now read the story carefully. Pay special attention to the idioms so that you're ready for Exercise 4.

4. Listen and Complete

Close your book. Listen to the story again. When the tape or your teacher pauses, try to complete the idiom.

5. Tell the Story

Cover the story and look at the pictures above. Tell the story using as many idioms as you can.

a. First, work with the whole class to retell the story.

b. Then tell the story to a partner or small group.

6. Answer the Questions

About the story . . . .

a. What are the disadvantages of Hoo's long hair? When does it come in handy?

b. What does Hoo have in common with his brother?

c. How often does Hoo wash his hair? Who gives him a hand?

d. How does Hoo keep warm when the weather is cool?

About you . . . .

e. Is your hair hard to take care of? Why or why not?

f. When do your friends give you a hand? When do you give them a hand?

g. What do you have in common with a member of your family?

7. Write About Yourself

Complete the sentences, writing something true about yourself.

a. Once in a blue moon, I _____.

b. On weekends, I usually put on _____. In cold

   weather, I put on _____.

c. I have many things in common with _____, such as

   _____.

d. When I get sick, I like to _____.

e. I take care of _____.

8. Write a Dialogue

Work with a partner. Write a dialogue using at least three idioms from the unit.
Act it out for a small group or the class.

9. Take a Dictation

_____

_____

_____

_____

10. Complete the Dialogue

a. Two young women, employees at a bookstore, are talking. Fill in the blanks with idioms from the box.

- in fact
- take ages
- give you a hand
- come in handy
- take care of
- according to

Let me (1)_____, Natasha.

Thanks! These boxes are really heavy. Why do we pack books in such large boxes?

Good question! You need a two-wheel dolly. It would (2)_____.

You're right. (3)_____, I think I saw one downstairs.

Let's go and get it.

Great idea! I have to (4)_____ a mountain of boxes. And they all have to be shipped out today, (5)_____ Ms. Chavez.

It will (6)_____ to move all these boxes! I'll tell Ms. Chavez I'm going to help you.

Thanks a lot, Julie.

b. Work with a partner. Role-play the dialogue together.

Review

A. Parts of the body: Many idioms use parts of the body. Complete these idioms and then match them to their meanings.

_e_ 1. have a _____*heart*_____ of gold ♡   a. be very expensive

____ 2. have cold _____ 👣   b. be afraid

____ 3. not believe one's _____ 👁 👁   c. help someone

____ 4. cost _____   d. be surprised

____ 5. give someone a _____   e. be very kind and generous

B. Odd one out: Cross out the word or phrase that doesn't go with the verb.

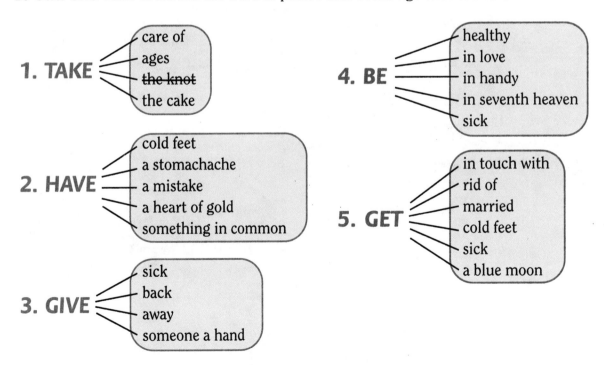

1. TAKE
- care of
- ages
- ~~the knot~~
- the cake

2. HAVE
- cold feet
- a stomachache
- a mistake
- a heart of gold
- something in common

3. GIVE
- sick
- back
- away
- someone a hand

4. BE
- healthy
- in love
- in handy
- in seventh heaven
- sick

5. GET
- in touch with
- rid of
- married
- cold feet
- sick
- a blue moon

C. *In, on, or out?* Complete each expression with the correct word.

1. come _____ handy

2. get _____ touch with

3. be _____ love

4. day in and day _____

5. _____ fact

6. once _____ a blue moon

7. work _____

8. put _____

9. _____ shape

10. _____ of shape

11. be _____ seventh heaven

D. *Good or bad?* Is the speaker feeling good or bad? Write the sentences in the correct boxes.

I'm as fit as a fiddle.
I'm in shape.
I'm running a fever.
I'm in love.

I have a stomachache.
I made a mistake.
I feel like a million dollars.

I'm out of shape.
I'm healthy.
I'm in seventh heaven.

E. Time expressions: Match the time expressions in A with their meanings in B. Draw lines. Then fill in the blanks below with the expressions in A.

A

1. at long last
2. right away
3. day in and day out
4. once in a blue moon
5. ages

B

a. rarely
b. a long time
c. finally
d. continually
e. immediately

It takes _____ to learn a new language. Some people think they can learn to speak _____. But, in fact, you really need to work hard and use the language _____ to become fluent. If you study just _____, you won't make much progress. When you master a language _____, you have the right to be very proud!

F. Group the idioms: What meaning associations do these expressions have? Put them into groups. (Note: Your answers may be slightly different from your classmates'.)

save up   as fit as a fiddle   give someone a hand
be in love   can afford   feel like a million dollars
in shape   get married   be in seventh heaven
work out   take care of   cost an arm and a leg
be healthy   give away   have a heart of gold
tie the knot

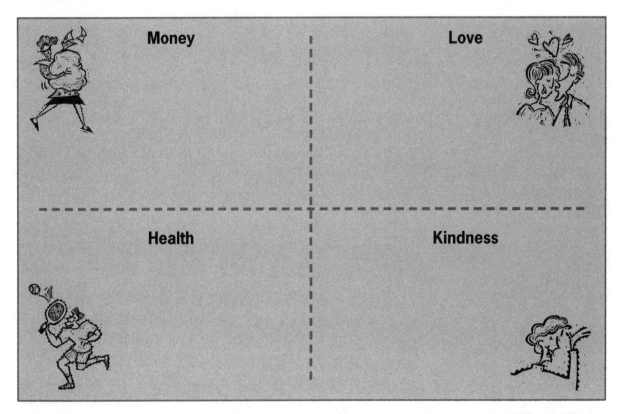

Money   Love

Health   Kindness

G. Two-line dialogues: Read each sentence in A and find an appropriate response in B.

A

__d__ 1. What's the matter?

_____ 2. Did he get married?

_____ 3. Can you afford those sunglasses?

_____ 4. This chair is heavy. I can't pick it up.

_____ 5. How often do you work out?

_____ 6. Berta tied the knot last week
        and didn't tell anyone.

B

a. I don't know. They cost an arm and a leg.

b. Once in a blue moon!

c. That really takes the cake!

d. I'm sick.

e. I'll give you a hand.

f. No, he got cold feet and put it off.

Now work with a partner. Read the two-line dialogues aloud, adding appropriate body language and intonation.

H. Idiom Game: Play this game in pairs or groups of three. Each player should put a different marker (a penny, a button, etc.) on START. Players will take turns, beginning with the person whose birthday comes first in the year.

Directions:

1. When it is your turn, close your eyes. Use your pencil to touch a number (in the box on the right). Move your marker that many spaces.
2. Try to make a **personal, true** sentence using the idiom.
3. If you can do it, stay on the space. If you can't, go back two spaces.
4. The first person to reach FINISH is the winner.

4	3	2	1	2
2	4	3	4	3
1	2	2	3	1

START	grow up	be in love	take it easy	take ages	keep on	be in seventh heaven

make a mistake	cost an arm and a leg	save up	get married	can't afford	in shape	tie the knot

have a heart of gold	right away	get in touch with	get cold feet	come in handy	get rid of	put off

work out	take care of	get sick	once in a blue moon	as fit as a fiddle	give away	cost an arm and a leg

day in and day out	be used to	have something in common with	give (someone) a hand	be healthy	get in touch with	senior citizen

FINISH	once in a blue moon	grow up	be used to	right away	out of shape	be in seventh heaven

Lost Skier Dances All Night Long

1. Quick Reading

Look at the pictures on page 27.
What is the story about?

Now read quickly to get the main idea.

LAYTON, UTAH, USA ¹It's the day before Christmas. Karen Hartley, 33, is skiing **by herself** at Powder Mountain in Utah. ²**By mistake**, she begins to ski off the trail. ³Soon she **gets lost**. She yells for help, but no one hears her. ⁴Night comes, and the temperature falls below freezing. Karen **is scared to death** and very cold. ⁵But she **keeps her head**. She plays music in her mind and dances **all night long** to stay warm. She dances to old disco songs, pop songs, and Christmas songs. "It was either dance or die," she said. "I **kept on** dancing. I didn't **give up**."

⁶The next morning, a helicopter begins to **look for** Karen. After 18 hours in the cold, she is rescued **in the nick of time**. ⁷Karen **is frozen stiff** but **all right**. ⁸She spends Christmas Day in a hot tub.

New idioms and expressions

all night long	during the entire night
by oneself	alone
by mistake	accidentally; because of a mistake
get lost	become unable to find one's way (home)
be scared to death	feel very afraid
keep one's head	stay calm in trouble or danger
keep on doing something*	continue doing something
give (something) up*	stop trying; quit something
look for someone or something*	try to find someone or something
in the nick of time	at the last possible moment; just before it's too late
be frozen stiff	be very cold
all right	fine; OK

*phrasal verb (see Lexicon and Appendix D)

2. Listen

Cover the story and look only at these pictures. Listen to the story two or three times.

3. Read the Story

Now read the story carefully. Pay special attention to the idioms so that you're ready for Exercise 4.

4. Listen and Complete

Close your book. Listen to the story again. When the tape or your teacher pauses, try to complete the idiom.

5. Tell the Story

Cover the story and look at the pictures above. Tell the story using as many idioms as you can.

a. First, work with the whole class to retell the story.

b. Then tell the story to a partner or small group.

6. Answer the Questions

About the story..

a. Is Karen skiing in a group?

b. What happens to her when she skies off the trail?

c. Karen is in a terrible situation. How does she feel?

d. What does she keep doing all night long?

e. What happens in the morning?

About you..

f. If you got lost in the mountains in winter, would you keep your head? What would you do to survive?

g. Tell about a time when you got lost. Where were you? Did someone look for you?

h. Tell about a time when you were scared to death. Were you with other people, or were you by yourself?

i. Tell about a dangerous or funny thing you did by mistake.

j. Do you like to dance? Did you ever dance all night long?

k. What kind of music do you like?

7. Write About Yourself

a. When I'm by myself, I like to _____.

b. I was scared to death once when _____.

c. I'm always looking for _____.

8. Write a Story

Write a story about a dangerous situation you were in. Use at least three idioms from the unit. Tell or read your story to a partner or group.

9. Take a Dictation

_____
_____
_____
_____
_____

10. Complete the Story

a. Read this true story and fill in the blanks with idioms from the box.

- all right
- by herself
- in the nick of time
- keeps her head
- is frozen stiff
- are looking for
- give up

Girl Uses Candy Wrappers to Find Father

Lake Creek, OR, USA   One day, Krystal Andrews, 17, and her father, Michael Andrews, 48, are riding in the mountains in a snowmobile. They (1)_____ animals. They're eating a bag of hard candies and **having a good time.***

Suddenly, the snowmobile hits some ice and turns over. It falls on top of Michael. He's injured and can't move. Krystal can't move the snowmobile either. She's scared to death, but she (2)_____. She puts several jackets around her father and begins to walk to their pickup truck (3)_____. As she walks, she drops candy wrappers to mark her route so that she can find her father again.

After about three miles (about five kilometers), she arrives at the truck. She drives to a store and calls 911. Rescuers come, and Krystal shows them the way to her father. They reach Michael Andrews (4)_____. He (5)_____ and has some broken ribs, but he's (6)_____. "I'm proud of Krystal. I knew she would not (7)_____. I knew she would save me," he says.

*have a good time: enjoy oneself

b. Read or tell the story to a partner.

Spaniards Paint the Town Red

7

1. Quick Reading

Look at the pictures on page 31.
What is the story about?

Now read quickly to get the main idea.

BUNYOL, SPAIN **¹Once a year**, the town of Bunyol in Spain **throws a** big **party**. The festival is called "La Tomatina." To **get ready**, townspeople put big plastic sheets over their windows. **²**By noon on the day of the festival, an enormous crowd gathers on the central square. **³**People shout, "Tomato! Tomato!" **at the top of their lungs**. They**'re dying to** see the tomatoes. **⁴**Just after 12:00 noon, the tomatoes arrive—in five big trucks! **⁵**Some people put on goggles. **⁶**The trucks dump the tomatoes, and the party begins. **⁷**People **go bananas**. They dive into the tomatoes and begin throwing them everywhere. **⁸Before long**, the square is a red, juicy pool. "It's wonderful to **let loose** and throw a big wet tomato at a neighbor," says Minerva Gonzalez of Bunyol. "Everyone **has a great time**."

New idioms and expressions

paint the town red	celebrate wildly
once a year	one time each year
throw a party	organize and have a party
get ready	prepare
at the top of one's lungs	very loudly
be dying to do something	want to do something very much
go bananas	become very excited and act wildly
before long	soon
let loose	act freely; release energy
have a great time	enjoy oneself very much

recycled idiom: put on   *phrasal verb (see Lexicon and Appendix D)

🔊 2. Listen

Cover the story and look only at these pictures. Listen to the story two or three times.

3. Read the Story

Now read the story carefully. Pay special attention to the idioms so that you're ready for Exercise 4.

🔊 4. Listen and Complete

Close your book. Listen to the story again. When the tape or your teacher pauses, try to complete the idiom.

5. Tell the Story

Cover the story and look at the pictures above. Tell the story using as many idioms as you can.

a. First, work with the whole class to retell the story.

b. Then tell the story to a partner or small group.

6. Answer the Questions

About the story . . . .

a. How often does the town of Bunyol throw this party?

b. What do people do to get ready?

c. What do people do just before noon?

d. What happens after the tomatoes arrive?

About you . . . .

e. Would you like to participate in La Tomatina? Why or why not?

f. Does your hometown have a festival where people go bananas? If so, tell the class about it. Does it happen once a year or more often?

g. Do you think it's a good idea for people to let loose sometimes? Why or why not?

h. Do you like to throw parties? Do your friends throw parties? Tell about a party you threw recently. How did you get ready for it?

i. What are you dying to do? Will you be able to do it before long?

7. Write About Yourself

Complete the sentences, writing something true about yourself.

a. I always have a great time when _____.

b. I'm dying to _____.

c. In my country, people usually paint the town red (when? where?) _____

_____.

8. Write a Story

Write a story about a wonderful party that you went to (or that you threw). Use at least four idioms from the unit. Tell your story to a partner or a small group.

9. Take a Dictation

_____

_____

_____

_____

_____

10. Complete the Dialogue

a. Two friends, Eduardo and Sara, are talking.
   Fill in the blanks with idioms from the box.

> • I'm dying to
> • paint the town red
> • throw a party
> • I'm getting ready
> • go bananas
> • once a year

Sara, are you doing anything for New Year's Eve?
Let's **go out*** and (1)_____.

Oh, no, sorry, Eduardo.
I can't. I don't have time.

What do you mean you don't have time?
New Year's comes just (2)_____.

I know, but I **have to**** study.
(3)_____
to take exams in January.

Oh, **come on!***** The Dance Club is going to
(4)_____. Everyone will be there.
(5)_____ go. Why don't you come with me?

I don't think so.

You work too hard. It's time to let loose.
Come on! Too much studying can make you
(6)_____.

* go out: leave the house for the purpose of entertainment

** have to: must

*** Come on!: Please do it! (informal)

Do you remember last year's party?
It was too wild. No, I prefer
to stay home with my books.

b. Work with a partner. Role-play the dialogue together.

Man Dances at His Own Funeral

8

1. Quick Reading

Look at the pictures on page 35.
What is the story about?

Now read quickly to get the main idea.

CAIRO, EGYPT ¹One day the police see a body on a beach in Egypt. The man is **dead as a doornail**. ²The ID cards in the man's wallet identify him as Ahmed Awadh, age 30.

³A short time later, Ahmed's friends and relatives are sitting in a funeral tent. They **feel blue** and they're crying over Ahmed. ⁴**All of a sudden**, the "dead" man walks into the tent, **looking like a million dollars**. ⁵His friends and family **are dumbfounded**. ⁶When they realize it's really Ahmed, they **go crazy**. They laugh, they cry, and they kiss him. ⁷Ahmed explains, "A thief **ripped** me **off** and took my ID cards. So when the police found the dead man, they thought he was me!" ⁸When Ahmed's friends and family **get over** their shock, the funeral **turns into** a party. They**'re on top of the world**! Police are still trying to identify the dead man.

New idioms and expressions

(as) dead as a doornail	completely dead
feel blue	be sad
all of a sudden	suddenly; unexpectedly
look like a million dollars/bucks	look healthy, happy, and attractive
be dumbfounded	be unable to speak because of shock or surprise
go crazy	become very excited and act wildly
rip someone or something off*	steal from someone; steal something
get over something*	recover from a physical illness or an emotional shock
turn into something*	become something different
be on top of the world	feel very happy

*phrasal verb (see Lexicon and Appendix D)

Cover the story and look only at these pictures. Listen to the story two or three times.

3. Read the Story

Now read the story carefully. Pay special attention to the idioms so that you're ready for Exercise 4.

■ **4. Listen and Complete**

Close your book. Listen to the story again. When the tape or your teacher pauses, try to complete the idiom.

5. Tell the Story

Cover the story and look at the pictures above. Tell the story using as many idioms as you can.

a. First, work with the whole class to retell the story.

b. Then tell the story to a partner or small group.

6. Answer the Questions

About the story...

a. Why do Ahmed's friends and family feel blue at the beginning of the story?

b. Why are they dumbfounded?

c. Why did the police think the dead man was Ahmed?

d. What does the funeral turn into?

e. How does everyone feel at the end of the story?

About you...

f. Has anyone ever ripped you off? What did they take?

g. Tell about a time when you felt blue. How did you get over it?

h. Tell about a time when you were dumbfounded. What happened?

i. What are funerals like in your country?

7. Write About Yourself

Complete the sentences, writing something true about yourself.

a. Sometimes I feel blue when ————————————————————.

b. I'm on top of the world when ————————————————————.

c. Sometimes I go crazy when ————————————————————.

8. Write a Dialogue

Work with a partner. Write a dialogue using at least three idioms from the unit.
Act it out for a small group or the class.

9. Take a Dictation

---

10. Complete the Dialogue

a. Two good friends, Jaime and Vlado, meet on the street. Fill in the blanks with idioms from the box.

- was dumbfounded
- get over
- look like a million bucks
- I'm feeling blue
- go crazy
- ripped off

Hey, Vlado. What's new?

Hey there, Jaime. Not too much. Is that a new jacket? It's great. You (1)_____.

It's **old as the hills.*** Someone (2)_____ my leather jacket, so I found this in my closet. How are things?

To tell the truth, (3)_____. Silvia **broke up with**** me last week.

Sorry to hear that, man.

I can't (4)_____ it. There was no reason. I (5)_____ when she told me it was over.

You need a vacation, Vlado. Leave town for a few days.

That's not a bad idea. If I keep thinking about Silvia, I'll (6)_____ .

* (as) old as the hills: very old

** break up with someone: end a love relationship

b. Work with a partner. Role-play the dialogue together.

Fish Turns the Tables on Fisherman

1. Quick Reading

Look at the pictures on page 39.
What is the story about?

Now read quickly to get the main idea.

KONAKOVO, RUSSIA ¹One day, a Russian man is fishing at a lake near Moscow. He **is crazy about** this sport. ²He catches a very large fish and **is on cloud nine**! ³Then he begins to **show off** for his pals. He grabs the fish and kisses it right on the mouth. ⁴But the fish **turns the tables on** the fisherman and bites his nose. ⁵It won't **let go**. The poor fisherman **is in hot water** now. "**Take it easy**," his friends advise. ⁶Then they have an idea. They **cut** the head **off** the fish. ⁷But the fish still won't let go of the fisherman's nose. It has strong teeth! ⁸Finally, doctors in a local hospital **set** the fisherman **free**. "**Play it safe**," they tell him. "Don't kiss any more fish!"

New idioms and expressions

turn the tables on someone	change a situation completely so that the unexpected happens
be crazy about someone or something	like someone or something very much
be on cloud nine	be very happy
show off (for someone)*	try to attract attention to oneself
let go (of someone or something)*	stop holding; release
be in hot water	be in a difficult situation; be in trouble
take it easy	stay calm; relax
cut something off*	remove something (often with a knife or scissors)
set someone or something free	liberate someone or something
play it safe	be careful; avoid danger

*phrasal verb (see Lexicon and Appendix D)

2. Listen

Cover the story and look only at these pictures. Listen to the story two or three times.

3. Read the Story

Now read the story carefully. Pay special attention to the idioms so that you're ready for Exercise 4.

4. Listen and Complete

Close your book. Listen to the story again. When the tape or your teacher pauses, try to complete the idiom.

5. Tell the Story

Cover the story and look at the pictures above. Tell the story using as many idioms as you can.

a. First, work with the whole class to retell the story.

b. Then tell the story to a partner or small group.

6. Answer the Questions

About the story . . . .

a. What is the Russian man crazy about?

b. What does he do to show off for his friends?

c. What happens next?

d. How do his friends try to help?

e. What do the doctors do? What do they tell the man?

About you . . . .

f. Do you like to fish? If so, are you crazy about it? Do you clean the fish?
   Do you cut the heads off?

g. What sports or hobbies are you crazy about?

h. Tell about a happy memory when you were on cloud nine.

i. Do you know people who show off? If so, what do they do?

j. Have you ever been in hot water? Why? When? Tell the story.

k. Are you the type of person who plays it safe, or do you like to take risks?
   Give an example.

7. Write About Yourself

Complete the sentences, writing something true about yourself.

a. I'm crazy about _____.

b. I'm on cloud nine when _____.

c. I usually try to play it safe when _____.

8. Write a Dialogue

Work with a partner. Write a dialogue using at least three idioms from the unit.
Act it out for a small group or the class.

9. Take a Dictation

_____

_____

_____

_____

_____

10. Complete the Dialogue

a. A young boy is talking to his older sister, Lupe.
   Fill in the blanks with idioms from the box.

- crazy about
- show off
- let go
- in hot water
- take it easy
- play it safe

Lupe, can you help me? I'm really (1)_____.

Again? You're always in some sort of trouble. You know, I'm not (2)_____ solving your problems all the time.

Come on! Please?

You're lucky I'm so nice. Maybe I'm too **softhearted***. What do you want?

Well, I was skating really fast, and, uh, I fell down.

Why do you always have to (3)_____ when you're skating? Did you hurt yourself?

No, but I was wearing Dad's watch and I ...

Oh, no! You didn't break Dad's watch, did you? His good watch? How stupid!

(4)_____! I'm going to buy him a new one. I'll (5)_____ and get him the most expensive one I can find. I just need your wallet. Thanks, Sis.

(6)_____ of that! I'm not giving you **a red cent.***

* be softhearted: be kind and sympathetic

** a red cent: a penny

recycled idiom: Come on!

b. Work with a partner. Role-play the dialogue together.

The Ringing Dog 10

1. Quick Reading

Look at the pictures on page 43.
What is the story about?

Now read quickly to get the main idea.

LONDON, ENGLAND **1**It's Christmas time in London. Rachel Murphy, 27, buys a Christmas gift for her roommate. It's a small cellular phone. **2**She wraps it and puts it under the Christmas tree in their apartment. **3A little bit later**, Rachel notices a pile of torn paper under the tree. The phone is gone! "**What's going on?**" she wonders. **4**She suspects Charlie, her roommate's dog, who **is sleeping like a log** near the tree. **5**She **looks high and low for** the phone, but it's nowhere. She can't **figure** it **out**. The phone **has vanished into thin air**!

6Rachel gets the phone number from the telephone company and dials the number. She hears ringing in Charlie's stomach. "**What in the world?**" she thinks. She's confused, but **all at once** she **gets the picture**. Charlie swallowed the phone! **7**She rushes the dog to the vet. "Don't worry," the vet says. "Just let nature take its course." **8Sure enough**, 24 hours later, the phone passes through Charlie's system. It seems to be in perfect working order!

New idioms and expressions

a little bit later ·	a short time later
What's going on? ·	What's happening?
sleep like a log ·	sleep very deeply
look high and low for ·	look everywhere for someone or something
someone or something	
figure something out* ·	solve a problem; understand something
vanish into thin air ·	disappear quickly and completely
What in the world? ·	What?; How strange! (an expression of shock or surprise)
all at once ·	suddenly; unexpectedly
get the picture ·	understand the situation or the facts
sure enough ·	as expected

*phrasal verb (see Lexicon and Appendix D)

⊟ **2. Listen**

Cover the story and look only at these pictures. Listen to the story two or three times.

3. Read the Story

Now read the story carefully. Pay special attention to the idioms so that you're ready for Exercise 4.

⊟ **4. Listen and Complete**

Close your book. Listen to the story again. When the tape or your teacher pauses, try to complete the idiom.

5. Tell the Story

Cover the story and look at the pictures above. Tell the story using as many idioms as you can.

a. First, work with the whole class to retell the story.

b. Then tell the story to a partner or small group.

6. Answer the Questions

About the story..

a. Where does Rachel look for the missing phone?

b. What is Charlie doing?

c. What can't Rachel figure out?

d. All at once, Rachel gets the picture. What happened to the phone?

About you...

e. Do you have a pet? If so, does it get into trouble like Charlie?

f. Did you ever own something that vanished into thin air? Did you look high and low for it? Did you ever find it?

g. Do you sleep like a log, or are you a light sleeper?

h. What is the best gift you ever received? On what holidays do you give gifts?

7. Write about Yourself

Complete the sentences, writing something true about yourself.

a. I used to have _____, but it/they vanished into thin air.

b. I often lose my _____, and have to look high and low for it/them.

c. Sometimes it's hard for me to figure out _____

_____.

8. Write a Dialogue

Work with a partner. Write a dialogue using at least three idioms from the unit. Act it out for a small group or the class.

9. Take a Dictation

10. Complete the Dialogue

a. A mother and her son, Troy, are talking.
   Fill in the blanks with idioms from the box.

> • a little bit later
> • what's going on
> • looking high and
>   low for
> • figure out
> • get the picture
> • vanish into thin air

Troy, (1)_____? I've been
(2)_____ you.

How come?*

You shouldn't (3)_____
when I ask you to do something. I told you
three times to wash the dishes.

Oh, Mom. Just a few more minutes. Just let me
(4)_____ this computer game.

Turn it off.

Can't I wash the dishes
(5)_____?

No, I said now. Do you want me
to unplug that computer?

Oh, Mom. Please?

Troy, **I'm at the end of my rope.****

OK, OK. I (6)_____.

* How come?: Why? (informal)

** be at the end of one's rope: be at the limit of one's patience

b. Work with a partner. Role-play the dialogue together.

Review

A. Idioms in pictures: What idioms do these pictures illustrate? Write the idioms in the blanks.

	IDIOM		MEANING

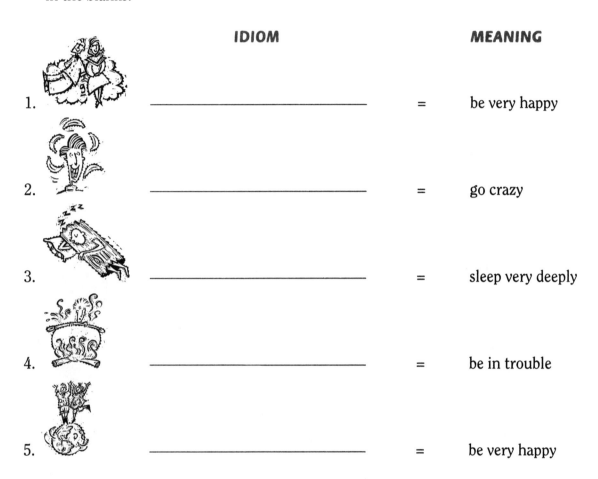

1. _____ = be very happy

2. _____ = go crazy

3. _____ = sleep very deeply

4. _____ = be in trouble

5. _____ = be very happy

B. Odd one out: Cross out the word or phrase that doesn't go with the verb.

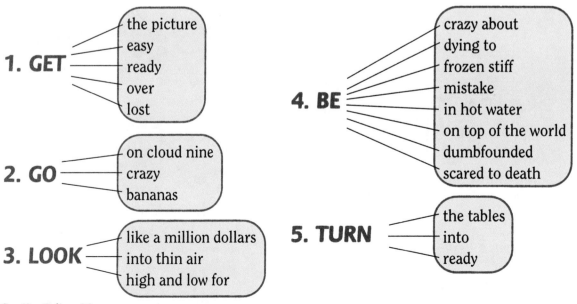

1. GET
- the picture
- easy
- ready
- over
- lost

2. GO
- on cloud nine
- crazy
- bananas

3. LOOK
- like a million dollars
- into thin air
- high and low for

4. BE
- crazy about
- dying to
- frozen stiff
- mistake
- in hot water
- on top of the world
- dumbfounded
- scared to death

5. TURN
- the tables
- into
- ready

C. In, on, or off? Complete each expression with the correct word.

1. What _____ the world?
2. turn the tables _____ someone
3. show _____ for someone
4. _____ the nick of time

5. What's going _____?
6. be _____ cloud nine
7. cut _____
8. be _____ top of the world

9. rip _____
10. be _____ hot water

D. Good or bad? Is the speaker feeling good or bad? Write the sentences in the boxes.

I'm on cloud nine.
I'm taking it easy.
I'm in hot water.
I look like a million dollars.

I'm frozen stiff.
I'm having a great time.
I'm scared to death.
I'm crazy about this food!

I'm really getting lost.
I feel blue.
I'm on top of the world.

E. Time expressions: Match the time expressions in A with their meanings in B. Draw lines. Then fill in the blanks below with the expressions in A.

A

1. before long
2. a bit later
3. all at once
4. once a year
5. in the nick of time
6. all night long

B

a. at the last possible moment
b. soon; a short time later
c. during the whole night
d. suddenly
e. one time each year
f. soon; a short time later

_____, in the summer, Igor travels from New York to see his family in Moscow.

On his last trip, Igor stayed up _____ to pack and get ready. When he arrived at

the airport, he went to the ticket counter to check in. _____, Igor realized that

his passport was at home. He knew he was in hot water, but he kept his head. He called his roommate

and asked him to bring his passport to the airport right away. _____ Igor heard an

announcement that his plane was boarding. _____, he heard another announcement,

"This is the final call for Flight 82 to Moscow." Igor was scared to death. But then he saw his roommate

running toward him. Igor made it onto the plane, just _____.

F. Crossword puzzle: Complete the idioms and fill in the crossword puzzle.

Across

3. I'm going to ____ a party Saturday night. Can you come?
5. The man was set ____ after ten years in prison.
7. My birthday comes only ____ a year, so I'm going to enjoy it!
9. I stayed up ____ night long.
11. Where's the dog? He vanished into thin ____!
13. Bob's in hot ____ with his boss because he's always late.

Down

1. I'm looking ____ my keys. Have you seen them?
2. Tina feels ____ because she's so far from home.
3. ____ it easy. Everything will be OK.
4. Let me cut ____ the price tag!
6. I didn't have time to get ____ for the test.
7. Somebody ripped me ____ on the subway. My money and credit cards are gone!
8. She loves to dance; in fact, she's ____ about it!
10. They really let ____ at the carnival.
12. Let's go out and paint the town ____!

G. Two-line dialogues: Read each sentence in A and find an appropriate response in B.

A		B

A

____ 1. How did you get lost?

____ 2. I'm getting ready to go to Paris.

____ 3. You look like a million dollars!

____ 4. I'm scared to death about the exam.

____ 5. You're going to the film by yourself?

B

a. Take it easy!

b. Yes. I'm dying to see it, and no one will go with me.

c. I took the wrong road by mistake.

d. Have a great time!

e. We're going to paint the town red tonight, so I bought a new dress.

Now work with a partner. Read the two-line dialogues aloud, adding appropriate body language and intonation.

H. Find someone who... Fill in the chart below with names of classmates. Try to write a different name in each blank. Stand up and walk around the room.
Ask questions such as:
   Are you crazy about cooking?
   Do you feel blue today?

Find someone who...

1. ...is crazy about cooking.

2. ...feels blue today.

3. ...is scared to death of spiders.

4. ...is on top of the world today.

5. ...likes to take it easy.

6. ...can keep his/her head in a crisis.

7. ...usually sleeps like a log.

8. ...often gets lost.

9. ...had a great time last weekend.

10. ...doesn't like to throw parties.

11. ...is dying to get married.

12. ...likes to let loose on weekends.

13. ...always plays it safe.

14. ...enjoys spending time by himself/herself.

Robber Chickens Out

11

1. Quick Reading

Look at the pictures on page 51.
What is the story about?

Now read quickly to get the main idea.

PEARL RIVER, NY, USA ¹In New York, nothing is surprising anymore. A man went into a bank in a town just north of New York City. He had a plastic bag over his head. ²He approached a teller and handed her a note. ³The teller **took a look at** the note. But she **couldn't make heads or tails of** it. The handwriting was terrible. ⁴She **excused herself** and went to consult with her co-workers. No one could read the note. ⁵Finally, one of the clerks figured out part of it. It said, "I have a gun." ⁶The clerks realized **at last** that the man was trying to **hold up** the bank. But when they looked up, the man with the bag on his head was gone. Apparently, he **lost his nerve** and **ran away**.

⁷Why didn't the teller react to the plastic bag on the man's head? She said only, "I thought maybe he had a skin problem." ⁸Police officers are still trying to **make sense of** the robber's note. "The note says he has a gun, but we have to **spend** more **time** studying the rest of it," said one officer.

New idioms and expressions

chicken out*	decide not to do something you planned because you're afraid
take a look at someone or something	look at someone or something quickly
cannot make heads or tails of something	not be able to understand something
excuse oneself	ask permission to leave a person or place
at last	finally; after a long time
hold someone or something up*	rob someone or something at gunpoint
lose one's nerve	become afraid and not do something
run away*	leave quickly; escape
make sense of something	understand something
spend time doing something	use time to do something

recycled idiom: figure out

*phrasal verb (see Lexicon and Appendix D)

2. Listen

Cover the story and look only at these pictures. Listen to the story two or three times.

3. Read the Story

Now read the story carefully. Pay special attention to the idioms so that you're ready for Exercise 4.

4. Listen and Complete

Close your book. Listen to the story again. When the tape or your teacher pauses, try to complete the idiom.

5. Tell the Story

Cover the story and look at the pictures above. Tell the story using as many idioms as you can.

a. First, work with the whole class to retell the story.

b. Then tell the story to a partner or small group.

6. Answer the Questions

About the story . . . .

a. What happened when the teller took a look at the note?

b. What did the clerks realize at last?

c. Why did the man run away?

d. What are police officers still trying to do?

About you . . . .

e. Tell about a time when you wanted to do something but you lost your nerve.

f. What do you like to spend time doing?

g. Did you ever visit a foreign country? If so, what was especially difficult to make sense of?

7. Write about Yourself

Complete the sentences, writing something true about yourself.

a. Sometimes I can't make sense of _____

_____.

b. I usually try to run away from _____

_____.

c. Once I wanted to _____, but
I chickened out.

8. Write a Dialogue

Work with a partner. Write a dialogue using at least three idioms from the unit.
Act it out for a small group or the class.

9. Take a Dictation

_____

_____

_____

_____

_____

Book 2

10. Complete the Dialogue

a. A husband and wife are talking. Fill in the blanks with idioms from the box.

- run away
- make sense of
- spend time
- take a look at
- at last
- chicken out

Guess what!* I'm writing a letter to my boss and asking for a raise.

Ah, (1)_____! **Good for you.**** You should have done it months ago.

I know. I always (2)_____. Oh, honey, where are you going? Don't (3)_____ yet.

How come?

I want you to (4)_____ my letter—you know, to see if you can (5)_____ it.

I'm in a hurry.** I want to get to the bank and the library before they close. I can (6)_____ helping you tonight. OK?

OK.

* Guess what!: a way of starting a conversation

** Good for you.: an expression of encouragement

*** be in a hurry: need to go somewhere quickly

recycled idiom: How come?

b. Work with a partner. Role-play the dialogue together.

Lovesick Elephant

1. Quick Reading

Look at the pictures on page 55.
What is the story about?

Now read quickly to get the main idea.

LYON, FRANCE [1]For Pankov and Mako, it was **love at first sight**. When the two elephants first saw each other in the Lyon zoo, they **fell head over heels in love**.

[2]For 34 years, the two elephants **looked after** each other and were happy. [3]Then one day, Mako got sick. He fell into a ditch by the elephants' cage. [4]A few months later, on a cold January day, he **passed away**.

[5]Pankov **was brokenhearted**. [6]**Over and over**, zookeepers tried to feed her, but she refused to eat. Although Pankov **had a sweet tooth**, she even refused her favorite treat, sweet spiced wine. Nothing could **cheer** her **up**. [7]Pankov didn't eat for four weeks, and she **went from bad to worse**. [8]On Valentine's Day, a month after Mako's death, zookeepers found Pankov in the same ditch. That night, she **died of a broken heart**.

New idioms and expressions

love at first sight	love that happens when two people first see each other
fall head over heels in love (with someone)	fall deeply and suddenly in love
look after someone or something*	take care of; watch over someone or something
pass away*	die
be brokenhearted	be very sad
over and over	repeatedly; many times
have a sweet tooth	love to eat sweet foods
cheer someone up*	make someone happier
go from bad to worse	go from a bad situation to a very bad situation
die of a broken heart	die from sadness

*phrasal verb (see Lexicon and Appendix D)

2. Listen

Cover the story and look only at these pictures. Listen to the story two or three times.

3. Read the Story

Now read the story carefully. Pay special attention to the idioms so that you're ready for Exercise 4.

4. Listen and Complete

Close your book. Listen to the story again. When the tape or your teacher pauses, try to complete the idiom.

5. Tell the Story

Cover the story and look at the pictures above. Tell the story using as many idioms as you can.
a. First, work with the whole class to retell the story.
b. Then tell the story to a partner or small group.

6. Answer the Questions

About the story...

a. What happened when Pankov and Mako first saw each other?

b. What did they do for 34 years?

c. What happened to Mako?

d. How did Pankov react?

e. How did zookeepers try to cheer her up?

f. What finally happened to Pankov?

About you...

g. Do you believe in love at first sight, or do you think true love grows over time?

h. Do you think animals have emotions?

i. Do you have a sweet tooth?

7. Write about Yourself

Complete the sentences, writing something true about yourself.

a. When I feel blue, ————————————————— usually cheer(s) me up.

b. When I was a child, ————————————————— looked after me.

c. I first fell head over heels in love (when, where, or with whom?) —————————

————————————————————————————————————.

8. Write a Dialogue

Work with a partner. Write a dialogue using at least three idioms from the unit.
Act it out for a small group or the class.

9. Take a Dictation

————————————————————————————————————

————————————————————————————————————

————————————————————————————————————

————————————————————————————————————

————————————————————————————————————

10. Complete the Dialogue

a. Two friends, Steve and Lucy, are talking.
   Fill in the blanks with idioms from the box.

> • look after
> • is going from bad to worse
> • fall head over heels in love
> • passed away
> • brokenhearted
> • cheer me up

Hey, Lucy. Why the **long face**?*

My boss (1)_____ last week.

Oh, I'm sorry to hear that! I know how much you liked her.

I'm (2)_____, Steve.

What will happen to your job? Who's going to (3)_____ the business?

The company is going to close. I'm going to lose my job. My financial situation (4)_____.

That's a lot of bad news. No wonder you're upset. But you'll find another job.

I hope so. Or better yet, maybe a millionaire will (5)_____ with me. That would (6)_____.

*long face: a sad look
recycled idiom: (it's) no wonder

b. Work with a partner. Role-play the dialogue together.

Shoplifter Gets a Dose of His Own Medicine

13

1. Quick Reading

Look at the pictures on page 59.
What is the story about?

Now read quickly to get the main idea.

SANTA FE, NM, USA **1**A man was driving his pickup truck from Colorado to New Mexico. It was **raining cats and dogs.** **2**The man saw a hitchhiker on the side of the road and **gave him a lift.** **3**The hitchhiker said his nickname was Tear Drop. Under his left eye was a tattoo in the shape of a tear drop.

4After a while, the driver **was hungry.** He stopped at Furr's Supermarket, leaving Tear Drop and his keys in the truck. **5**In the supermarket he took several packages of cookies and chips and hid them in his coat pockets. **In a hurry,** he walked toward the exit without paying. **6**But the store manager **caught him red-handed.** "I saw you **shoplift.** "Give me that food," he said. **7**The manager then escorted him out of the supermarket.

8They came out **just in time** to see Tear Drop **taking off** in the pickup. The police are still looking for Tear Drop.

New idioms and expressions

get a dose of one's own medicine	get the same bad treatment you give other people
rain cats and dogs	rain very hard
give someone a lift	give someone a ride in a car or truck
after a while	later; a short time later
be hungry	have an appetite; want to eat
in a hurry	rushed; need to move quickly
catch someone red-handed	catch someone who is committing a crime
shoplift (something)	steal (something) from a store
(just) in time	(just) before the last minute; (just) before the deadline
take off*	leave a place (by car, on foot, or by plane)

*phrasal verb (see Lexicon and Appendix D)

2. Listen

Cover the story and look only at these pictures. Listen to the story two or three times.

3. Read the Story

Now read the story carefully. Pay special attention to the idioms so that you're ready for Exercise 4.

4. Listen and Complete

Close your book. Listen to the story again. When the tape or your teacher pauses, try to complete the idiom.

5. Tell the Story

Cover the story and look at the pictures above. Tell the story using as many idioms as you can.

a. First, work with the whole class to retell the story.

b. Then tell the story to a partner or small group.

6. Answer the Questions

About the story . . . .

a. How was the weather when Tear Drop was trying to get a lift?

b. Why did the driver stop at the supermarket?

c. Why was the driver in a hurry in the supermarket?

d. How did he feel when he saw Tear Drop taking off in his pickup?

e. Explain the title of the story.

About you . . . .

f. Do you have a car or a pickup truck? Do you sometimes give friends a lift? Do your friends give you a lift?

g. Have you ever given a lift to a hitchhiker? Do you think this is a good idea?

h. Do you have a nickname? What is it? Do you like your nickname? How did you get it?

i. Are you often in a hurry? Why/why not? Do you think Americans are in a hurry?

j. Have you ever been the victim of a crime? If so, what happened?

7. Write about Yourself

Complete the sentences, writing something true about yourself.

a. I plan to _____ after a while.

b. When I'm really hungry, _____.

c. I'm in a hurry to _____.

8. Finish the Story

Work with a partner. Write an ending to the story. What happened to Teardrop? What happened to the shoplifter? Use at least three idioms from the unit.

9. Take a Dictation

_____

_____

_____

_____

_____

10. Complete the Dialogue

a. Two friends, Mei and Jill, are getting ready to leave work at the end of the day. Fill in the blanks with idioms from the box.

> - a while
> - I'm hungry
> - raining cats and dogs
> - in a hurry
> - give me a lift
> - just in time

Jill, I was looking for you! Can you (1) _____ home?

Oh, sure, Mei. You found me (2) _____. I'm leaving right now.

Thanks a lot. It's (3) _____ out there.

Wow, you're right! What a downpour! My pickup is right there. Let's **run for it!***

This rain is **the pits.****

Yeah, it's awful. I'll turn on the heater. You'll warm up after (4) _____. We could stop at Bob's Burgers if you're not (5) _____ They have a drive-through window.

Great idea! I didn't have time to eat lunch today, so (6) _____.

* run for it: run quickly for safety (informal)

** the pits: very, very bad (slang)

b. Work with a partner. Role-play the dialogue together.

14

Crow Commits Crime

1. Quick Reading

Look at the pictures on page 63.
What is the story about?

Now read quickly to get the main idea.

CLEARWATER, FL, USA ¹One day, when Frank Landstrom was playing golf in Clearwater, Florida, something strange happened. His $450 gold bracelet was in his golf cart. ²All of a sudden, a big crow flew down **out of nowhere** and grabbed the bracelet. ³"What in the world?" Frank thought. He watched **wide-eyed** as the crow **made off with** his bracelet. ⁴Frank **was in a bad mood** because he was sure the bracelet was gone **for good**.

⁵Later that day, a man named Tom Johnson **pulled into** a supermarket parking lot 35 miles from Clearwater. Something shiny on the ground **caught his eye**. ⁶He picked it up. It was a gold bracelet!

⁷The next morning, Tom saw a story in the newspaper about a crow and a gold bracelet. He **put two and two together**. ⁸Then he got in touch with Frank Landstrom to give the bracelet back. Frank couldn't believe his luck. He was thrilled to **get** it **back**.

New idioms and expressions

out of nowhere	suddenly and unexpectedly
wide-eyed	very surprised
make off with something*	take or steal something
be in a bad mood	feel angry or sad
for good	forever; permanently
pull into a place*	drive one's car into a place
catch one's eye	attract one's attention
put two and two together	figure something out from what one sees, hears, learns, etc.
get something back*	receive something that belonged to you before

recycled idioms: all of a sudden, give back, What in the world?, pick up, get in touch with

*phrasal verb (see Lexicon and Appendix D)

2. Listen

Cover the story and look only at these pictures. Listen to the story two or three times.

3. Read the Story

Now read the story carefully. Pay special attention to the idioms so that you're ready for Exercise 4.

4. Listen and Complete

Close your book. Listen to the story again. When the tape or your teacher pauses, try to complete the idiom.

5. Tell the Story

Cover the story and look at the pictures above. Tell the story using as many idioms as you can.

a. First, work with the whole class to retell the story.

b. Then tell the story to a partner or small group.

6. Answer the Questions

About the story...

a. Why did the crow make off with the bracelet, in your opinion?

b. Why was Frank in a bad mood?

c. Where was Tom Johnston when the bracelet caught his eye?

d. When did he put two and two together?

e. Do you think Tom's an unusual man? Why or why not?

About you...

f. Tell about a time when you lost something valuable. Did you ever get it back, or was it gone for good?

g. Have you ever found something valuable? Did you try to give it back to the owner?

h. Are you in a bad or a good mood today? Why?

i. Do you know an unusual story about an animal? If so, tell it.

7. Write about Yourself

Complete the sentences, writing something true about yourself.

a. I'm in a bad mood when _____.

b. Once I had a/an _____, but it's gone for good.

c. I'm wide-eyed when I see _____.

8. Write a Dialogue

Work with a partner. Write a dialogue using at least three idioms from the unit. Act it out for a small group or the class.

9. Take a Dictation

_____
_____
_____
_____
_____

10. Complete the Dialogue

a. Read this true story and fill in the blanks with idioms from the box.

> - was in a bad mood
> - for good
> - caught his eye
> - pulled into
> - made off with
> - wide-eyed

Twenty-Five Years Later, Man Says He's Sorry

Bradgate, IA, USA When Dale Wagner was a young man in Bradgate, Iowa, he had a canoe. He kept it behind his house. One day he went to get the canoe, but it wasn't there. Someone had (1)_____ it! Wagner was sure the canoe was gone (2)_____. He (3)_____ when he went to report the crime to the police.

Twenty-five years later, the post office in Bradgate received an envelope addressed to the postmaster. There was $150 in the envelope. There was also a letter. The letter writer said that twenty-five years ago he worked on a train that (4)_____ Bradgate. A canoe (5)_____ and he took it. "I am not proud of what I did. Please give the money to the owner of the canoe if you can find him."

Someone in town remembered that the canoe **belonged to*** Dale Wagner. When Wagner got the envelope, he was (6)_____. "I was really surprised. This restored my faith in human beings."

*belong to someone: be the property of someone

b. Read or tell the story to a partner.

On the Cutting Edge

15

1. Quick Reading

Look at the pictures on page 67.
What is the story about?

Now read quickly to get the main idea.

SEATTLE, WA, USA [1]Do you like to hike? Climb mountains? Ride a mountain bike? [2]Did you know that people in Seattle can do all these things *indoors*, in the middle of the city? REI, a superstore that sells equipment for outdoor activities, entertains and educates people as they shop.

[3]Do you want to buy hiking boots? You can **try** them **on**, of course, as at any other store. But at REI, you can also **try** them **out** on a man-made hiking trail. [4]If you**'re interested in** buying a waterproof jacket, you can put it on and walk into a man-made rainstorm to **make sure** it really keeps you dry! [5]If you want to try out a mountain bike, there's a Mountain Bike Test Trail around the store. [6]**The icing on the cake** is a 64-foot climbing wall where shoppers can test climbing equipment.

[7]This hands-on store is very popular, and it**'s making** a lot of **money**. "I like to **go shopping** here," says one customer. "It's fun." [8]The Seattle store is changing the whole idea of shopping. It **is on the cutting edge** of retail marketing in the United States, and experts say more stores will soon **follow in its footsteps**.

New idioms and expressions

be on the cutting edge (of something)	be the leader (in a certain field)
try something on*	test the fit of shoes or clothes
try something out*	test something to see how it works
be interested in something	want to do or have something
make sure	check something yourself to be sure about it
the icing on the cake	the best part
make money	make a profit; earn money
go shopping	shop
follow in someone's footsteps	follow someone's example

recycled idiom: put on   *phrasal verb (see Lexicon and Appendix D)

2. Listen

Cover the story and look only at these pictures. Listen to the story two or three times.

3. Read the Story

Now read the story carefully. Pay special attention to the idioms so that you're ready for Exercise 4.

4. Listen and Complete

Close your book. Listen to the story again. When the tape or your teacher pauses, try to complete the idiom.

5. Tell the Story

Cover the story and look at the pictures above. Tell the story using as many idioms as you can.

a. First, work with the whole class to retell the story.

b. Then tell the story to a partner or small group.

6. Answer the Questions

About the story...

a. How is buying boots at REI different from buying them at other stores?

b. What can you do if you're interested in testing a waterproof jacket?

c. What is the icing on the cake at REI?

d. How do customers feel about the store?

e. How is it doing financially? Can you give some reasons?

f. Would you be interested in shopping at REI? Why or why not?

About you..

g. Are you interested in outdoor activities? If so, which ones?

h. Tell about a wonderful vacation you had. What was the icing on the cake?

i. Is making a lot of money important to you? What do you think is the best way to make a lot of money?

j. Do you know of other businesses that are on the cutting edge?

k. Would you like to start a business? If so, what kind?

7. Write About Yourself

Complete the sentences, writing something true about yourself.

a. I'm interested in _____.

b. I like to go shopping at _____ because

_____ .

c. I hope that I can follow in _____'s footsteps because

_____ .

8. Write an Ad

Work with a partner. Write and illustrate a magazine advertisement for REI or another store. Use at least three idioms from the unit.

9. Take a Dictation

_____

_____

_____

_____

_____

10. Complete the Ad

This is an advertisement for a tropical hotel and resort. Fill in the blanks with idioms from the box.

- **try out**
- **go shopping**
- **the icing on the cake**
- **I'm interested in**
- **spend time on**

THE Vacation OF YOUR DREAMS

- Fine food
- Beautiful beaches
- Luxury accommodations

Tropical Paradise Resort has it all! Our friendly hospitality is

(1) _____

(2) _____ swimming and relaxing on our white sandy beaches.

(3) _____ in our 20 shops and boutiques.

(4) _____ our sailboats and jet skis.

For more information, please send this coupon to Tropical Paradise Resort, PO Box 818, San Juan, Puerto Rico 00937

Yes, (5) _____ learning more about Tropical Paradise Resort. Please send me photos and price information.

Name: _____

Address: _____

A. Parts of the body: Many idioms use parts of the body. Complete these idioms. Then match them to their meanings.

____ 1. have a sweet _____   a. pass away because of sadness

____ 2. die of a broken _____   b. attract one's attention

____ 3. fall _____ over _____ in love   c. love to eat candy and cakes

____ 4. catch someone red-_____   d. very surprised

____ 5. catch someone's_____   e. begin to love suddenly and deeply

____ 6. wide-_____   f. find someone doing something wrong

B. Expressions with *be, go,* and *make*: What expressions can you make with *be, go,* and *make*? Put a check (✓) in the correct boxes.

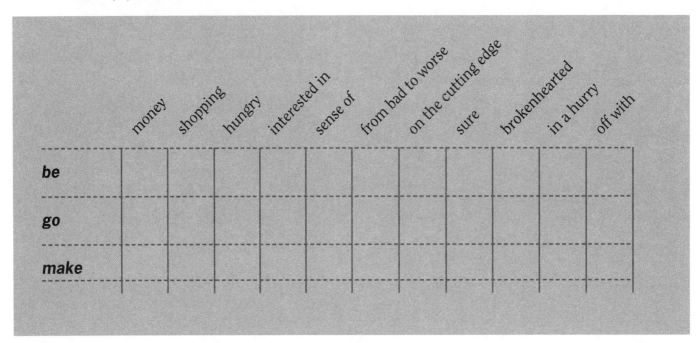

	money	shopping	hungry	interested in	sense of	from bad to worse	on the cutting edge	sure	brokenhearted	in a hurry	off with
be											
go											
make											

C. On, out, up, or away? Complete the sentences with the correct words.

1. The robber tried to hold _____ the bank. But in the end, he chickened _____ and
   ran _____ .

2. Zookeepers tried to cheer Pankov _____ , but they couldn't. She wouldn't eat after
   Mako passed _____ .

3. At REI, you can try _____ boots as in any other shoe store. But you can also try
   them _____ on their hiking test trail.

D. Group the idioms: Put the idioms into categories based on meaning.
   (Note: Your answers may be slightly different from your classmates'.)

chicken out	**wide-eyed**	**be brokenhearted**
can't make heads or tails of	**can't make sense of**	**run away**
What in the world?	**be in a bad mood**	**lose one's nerve**
die of a broken heart		

Confusion or surprise	Fear	Sadness or depression

E. Time expressions: Complete each sentence with one of the following expressions.

for good	**at last**	**all of a sudden**
over and over	**just in time**	**after a while**

1. Jane watched the movie on video _____ . Even after seeing it five
   times, she wasn't tired of it.

2. I got to the bus stop _____ ! The bus was taking off, but the driver
   let me on.

3. Juan says he's going to live in New York _____ . He'll never move
   again.

4. I'll do my homework _____ . I want to watch TV for an hour first.

5. I feel sick _____ . I'm going to lie down for a few minutes.

6. Harold was looking for a good used car for a long time, and he found one
   _____ .

F. Matching: Match A with the pictures in B to make complete expressions. Draw lines. Then fill in the blanks with the missing words.

A

1. rain cats and _____

2. the icing on the _____

3. follow in someone's _____

4. spend _____

5. get a dose of one's own _____

6. make _____

7. love at first _____

B

a.

b.

c.

d.

e.

f.

g.

G. Separable phrasal verbs: *cheer up, hold up, get back, try on, try out*

When a phrasal verb is separable, separation is optional (not necessary) when the direct object is a noun.
CORRECT: *Zookeepers tried to cheer up Pankov.*
CORRECT: *Zookeepers tried to cheer Pankov up.*

Separation is obligatory (necessary) when the direct object is a pronoun.
CORRECT: *Zookeepers tried to cheer her up.*
INCORRECT: *Zookeepers tried to cheer up her.*

Rewrite each sentence two ways: first using a noun, then using a pronoun.

1. The robber tried to hold up the bank.

_____

_____

2. Frank Landstrom was happy to get back his gold bracelet.

_____

_____

3. At REI, you can try on hiking boots.

_____

_____

4. You can also try out boots on the test trail.

_____

_____

H. Idiom Game: Play this game in pairs or groups of three. Each player should put a different marker (a penny, a button, etc.) on START. Players will take turns, beginning with the person whose birthday comes first in the year.

Directions:

1. When it is your turn, close your eyes. Use your pencil to touch a number (in the box on the right). Move your marker that many spaces.
2. Try to make a **personal, true** sentence using the idiom.
3. If you can do it, stay on the space. If you can't, go back two spaces.
4. The first person to reach FINISH is the winner.

4	3	2	1	2
2	4	3	4	3
1	2	2	3	1

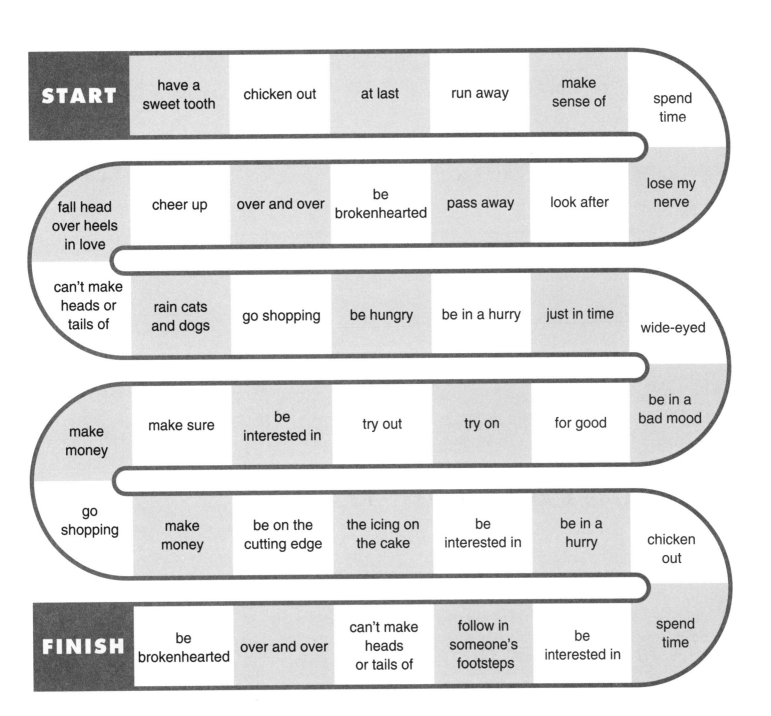

Man Tries to Turn Over a New Leaf

1. Quick Reading

Look at the pictures on page 75.
What is the story about?

Now read quickly to get the main idea.

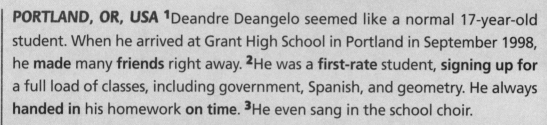

PORTLAND, OR, USA **1**Deandre Deangelo seemed like a normal 17-year-old student. When he arrived at Grant High School in Portland in September 1998, he **made** many **friends** right away. **2**He was a **first-rate** student, **signing up for** a full load of classes, including government, Spanish, and geometry. He always **handed in** his homework **on time**. **3**He even sang in the school choir.

4But three months later, police interrupted the choir practice and arrested Deangelo **on the spot**. **5It turns out that** he was not 17; he was 31! And his real name was not Deangelo, but Michael Backman. Backman had forged documents to change his identity and become a high school student again. **6**He was trying to hide from police for many different crimes.

7Grant High School was the school that Backman attended 13 years earlier. He wanted to **turn over a new leaf**. "I was trying to return to a time when I was not a criminal, to start again, to get a scholarship and go to college," he told police. **8**Backman is now **behind bars** for his new crime **as well as** his old ones.

New idioms and expressions

turn over a new leaf · · · · · · · · · · · · · · · ·	decide to improve your behavior
make friends · · · · · · · · · · · · · · · · · · ·	become friendly with other people
first-rate ·	excellent
sign up for something* · · · · · · · · · · · ·	agree to do something by writing your name
hand something in* · · · · · · · · · · · · · ·	give something that is due to someone
on time ·	at the arranged time; not late
on the spot · · · · · · · · · · · · · · · · · · ·	at that exact time and place
it turns out that · · · · · · · · · · · · · · · ·	what is finally clear is that
behind bars · · · · · · · · · · · · · · · · · · ·	in prison
as well as ·	and also; in addition to

recycled idiom: right away   *phrasal verb (see Lexicon and Appendix D)

2. Listen

Cover the story and look only at these pictures. Listen to the story two or three times.

3. Read the Story

Now read the story carefully. Pay special attention to the idioms so that you're ready for Exercise 4.

4. Listen and Complete

Close your book. Listen to the story again. When the tape or your teacher pauses, try to complete the idiom.

5. Tell the Story

Cover the story and look at the pictures above. Tell the story using as many idioms as you can.

a. First, work with the whole class to retell the story.

b. Then tell the story to a partner or small group.

6. Answer the Questions

a. Why did Backman change his name and return to Grant High School?

b. What did he do when he first arrived at the school?

c. What kind of student was he? Did he do his homework?

d. What did police do when they came into the school?

e. Where is Backman now? Is this the right place for him?

About you..

f. Do you sometimes feel that you should turn over a new leaf? If so, what do you want to change about your life?

g. Is it easy to make new friends in your school or town? How do you do it?

h. Do you want to sign up for a class in the future? Which one(s)?

i. Do you always hand in your homework on time?

7. Write about Yourself

Complete the sentences, writing something true about yourself.

a. I am a first-rate _____.

b. I always _____ on time.

c. I used to think _____,

but it turns out that _____.

8. Write a Dialogue

Work with a partner. Write a dialogue using at least three idioms from the unit. Act it out for a small group or the class.

9. Take a Dictation

10. Complete the Dialogue

a. Two friends are talking. Fill in the blanks with idioms from the box.

- first-rate
- as well as
- on the spot
- turn over a new leaf
- am signing up for
- it turns out that
- on time

Hi, Ramona. How did your job interview go?

Terrific. You won't believe this! I was hired (1) _____!

Incredible! You're so lucky! Aviron is a (2) _____ company. Are there good benefits?

Yes, I (3) _____ a very good health plan. And (4) _____ they'll provide health coverage for my husband (5) _____ day care for my son.

That's great.

There's only one problem. I have to start work at 8:00. You know how I hate getting up early. I was never (6) _____ at my last job — and we didn't start till 9:00.

You'll have to (7) _____. And get a good alarm clock!

b. Work with a partner. Role-play the dialogue together.

17
Gorilla Lends a Helping Hand

1. Quick Reading

Look at the pictures on page 79.
What is the story about?

Now read quickly to get the main idea.

CHICAGO, IL, USA ¹Binti-Jua is a fierce-looking gorilla who lives at the Brookfield Zoo in Chicago. One day, she was sitting in the gorilla habitat eating bananas. ²A little boy and his mother were watching the gorillas. ³All at once, the child climbed over the stone wall. "**Look out!**" someone shouted. ⁴But it was too late. The child fell 24 feet onto the cement floor of the gorilla habitat and **was knocked out cold**.

⁵With her own baby on her back, Binti-Jua picked up the young boy. ⁶"The gorilla's got my baby!" cried the boy's mother. Onlookers **were scared out of their wits**. "I feared the worst," said one paramedic. "I thought she was going to treat him like a toy." ⁷But Binti-Jua was **cool as a cucumber** as she took care of the boy. She rocked him in her arms and **kept** the other gorillas **away**. ⁸Then she carried him to the gate where zoo officials were waiting. "I can't believe how gentle she was! We**'re proud of** her. She**'s the apple of our eye**," said a zoo director. The little boy is **safe and sound**, and Binti-Jua is a hero.

24 feet = 7.2 meters

New idioms and expressions

lend (someone) a (helping) hand	help (someone)
Look out!*	Be careful!; Be alert!
be knocked out cold	become unconscious from a blow to the head
be scared out of one's wits	be very afraid
(as) cool as a cucumber	very calm and relaxed
keep (someone or something) away*	make (someone or something) stay at a distance
be proud of someone or something	be very pleased with someone or something
be the apple of one's eye	be one's favorite person or thing
safe and sound	safe and healthy; with no damage or injury

recycled idioms: pick up, take care of, all at once   *phrasal verb (see Lexicon and Appendix D)

2. Listen

Cover the story and look only at these pictures. Listen to the story two or three times.

3. Read the Story

Now read the story carefully. Pay special attention to the idioms so that you're ready for Exercise 4.

4. Listen and Complete

Close your book. Listen to the story again. When the tape or your teacher pauses, try to complete the idiom.

5. Tell the Story

Cover the story and look at the pictures above. Tell the story using as many idioms as you can.

a. First, work with the whole class to retell the story.

b. Then tell the story to a partner or small group.

6. Answer the Questions

About the story..

a. What happened to the boy when he fell into the gorilla habitat?

b. How did onlookers feel?

c. How did Binti-Jua act? How did she lend a helping hand?

d. How does the zoo director feel about Binti-Jua?

About you..

e. Do you approve of putting animals in zoos? Why or why not?

f. Tell about a time when you were scared out of your wits.

g. When you take a test, are you nervous or cool as a cucumber?

h. Were you ever knocked out cold? If so, how did it happen?

i. Who (or what) is the apple of your eye?

j. What accomplishment in your life are you proud of?

7. Write about Yourself

Complete the sentences, writing something true about yourself.

a. I often lend _____ a hand _____

   because _____.

b. I'm very proud of _____

c. I'm the apple of _____'s eye.

8. Write a Dialogue

Work with a partner. Write a dialogue using at least three idioms from the unit.
Act it out for a small group or the class.

9. Take a Dictation

_____

_____

_____

_____

_____

10. Complete the Story

a. Read the true story and fill in the blanks with idioms from the box.

> • **look out**
> • **lend him a hand**
> • **safe and sound**
> • **scared out of his wits**
> • **the apple of her eye**

Boy Survives Fall Over Cliff

Encinitas, CA, USA Grant Taylor Huff is an active two-year-old boy. His grandmother often takes care of him. He's
(1) _____.

One day, Grant was in the backyard of his grandmother's home, which sits above the Pacific Ocean. He was playing with his four-year-old cousin. Grant began to climb over a wall. "(2) _____!" his cousin called. But it was too late. Grant fell and rolled down a steep hill for 30 feet (9 meters). Then he flew off a cliff toward the ocean, 50 feet (15 meters) below.

A couple was walking on the beach when they saw something fall from the sky. They found little Grant in the water, just as large waves began to **wash over*** him. They ran to
(3) _____. When they pulled Grant out of the water, he was (4) _____ but seemed unhurt. The couple contacted the police, and Grant was returned to his family (5) _____.

*wash over: cover with water
recycled idiom: take care of

b. Read or tell the story to a partner.

Money Rains from the Sky

1. Quick Reading

Look at the pictures on page 83.
What is the story about?

Now read quickly to get the main idea.

MIAMI, FL, USA [1]Early one morning, residents in a very poor neighborhood in Miami heard a loud crash. An armored truck had smashed into a guard rail and overturned on a bridge. The truck was carrying millions of dollars. [2]The doors of the truck burst open, and bags of money fell out. The bags broke open, and money flew **all over the place**. [3]Hundreds of people rushed to **get their hands on** the cash. "Money is raining from the sky!" they shouted. Altogether, the people stuffed $500,000 into their pockets and bags.

[4]When the excitement **died down**, the police went from house to house and announced, "If you took money, you must give it back within 48 hours." [5]They waited at the police station, but **in the end** only two people **showed up**—a woman and a boy. The woman **turned in** $19.53, and the boy, Herbert Tarvin, 11, turned in the 85 cents he picked up.

[6]Herbert's honesty **made an impression on** people. When officials at Disney World in Orlando, Florida, **found out** about Herbert, they invited him and his entire class to **take a trip** there. [7]When they arrived, the Disney company **rolled out the red carpet** for the 16 children. [8]Herbert and his friends **had the time of their lives**. "We like to reward kids for good behavior," a Disney spokesperson commented.

New idioms and expressions

all over the place · · · · · · · · · · · · · · · · · · ·	everywhere
get one's hands on something · · · · · · · ·	take ahold of something
die down* ·	come slowly to an end; grow weaker
in the end ·	after all; ultimately
show up* ·	arrive; appear
turn something in* · · · · · · · · · · · · · · · ·	give something to someone
make an impression (on someone) · · · ·	have a memorable effect (on someone)
find something out* · · · · · · · · · · · · · · ·	learn; discover something
take a trip ·	travel someplace
roll out the red carpet (for someone) · ·	welcome an important guest with special treatment
have the time of one's life · · · · · · · · · · ·	have a wonderful time

recycled idiom: give back   *phrasal verb (see Lexicon and Appendix D)

2. Listen

Cover the story and look only at these pictures. Listen to the story two or three times.

3. Read the Story

Now read the story carefully. Pay special attention to the idioms so that you're ready for Exercise 4.

4. Listen and Complete

Close your book. Listen to the story again. When the tape or your teacher pauses, try to complete the idiom.

5. Tell the Story

Cover the story and look at the pictures above. Tell the story using as many idioms as you can.
a. First, work with the whole class to retell the story.
b. Then tell the story to a partner or small group.

6. Answer the Questions

About the story...

a. When the truck crashed, what flew all over the place?

b. What did people do?

c. What happened when the excitement died down?

d. How many people showed up at the police station? What did they turn in?

e. What happened when Disney World found out about Herbert?

f. In your opinion, why did only two people turn in money?

About you...

g. Do you want to take a trip? Where? Why?

h. Tell about an occasion when you had the time of your life.

i. When you meet someone new, what makes an impression on you?

j. What time do you usually show up for class?

7. Write about Yourself

Complete the sentences, writing something true about yourself.

a. I took a trip to _____ last year because

_____.

b. I would like to get my hands on _____.

c. I had the time of my life (when? where?) _____

_____.

8. Write a Dialogue

Work with a partner. Write a dialogue using at least three idioms from the unit.
Act it out for a small group or the class.

9. Take a Dictation

_____

_____

_____

_____

_____

10. Complete the Dialogue

a. Two friends, Rashida and Gladys, are talking. Fill in the blanks with idioms from the box.

> - **all over the place**
> - **took a trip**
> - **rolled out the red carpet**
> - **made a big impression on**
> - **found out**
> - **had the time of my life**

Gladys, where have you been? I've been looking for you!

I was gone. I (1)_____ to China.

China? **My goodness!*** How was it?

The greatest. I (2)_____. You know I studied Chinese for two years. Well, I've always wanted to visit China.

Where in China did you go?

We went (3)_____: the Great Wall, Beijing, Shanghai, Xian. I went with a tour group. They really (4)_____ for us. And the best was that I spoke a lot of Chinese. I (5)_____ that people can understand me!

Wow! What did you think of the Great Wall?

It's amazing. It (6)_____ me. It's the largest man-made structure in the world. Did you know that?

*My goodness!: an exclamation of surprise

b. Work with a partner. Role-play the dialogue together.

Janitor's Dream Comes True

19

1. Quick Reading

Look at the pictures on page 87.
What is the story about?

Now read quickly to get the main idea.

LAS CRUCES, NM, USA Primo Torres has learned that dreams can **come true**. **1**Born in Juárez, Mexico, Torres grew up in Texas in a poor family. **2**As a child, Torres **was a bookworm** and he loved school. At 15, he already **dreamed of** being a teacher.

3One day at school, young Torres **dropped by** to see his guidance counselor. He told the counselor his plans for the future. "But this guy said, 'Primo, you will never be college material,'" Torres said. "When he told me that, I gave up. He **threw cold water on** my dream."

4After graduating from high school, Torres got a job as a janitor at Mayfield High School in Las Cruces, New Mexico. He cleaned bathrooms and swept floors. **5**The years **went by**. **Now and then**, he talked to his wife about his childhood dream of being a teacher.

6One day, when Torres was 41 years old, his wife gave him some papers. She had enrolled him in college! "It was strange **going back** to school at my age," said Torres. "I felt like an old man around all those kids!" **7**The words of his first professor changed his life. "Everyone in this room **is capable of** succeeding. You can all **make an A**," he said. Torres **hit the books** and made his first A in college.

8Torres finished college, and now he's teaching at Mayfield High School. His students love him. "Many students don't realize that I'm the same man who used to sweep the floors in this school," said Torres.

New idioms and expressions

come true ·	become real; change from dream to fact
be a bookworm · · · · · · · · · · · · · · · · · ·	love to read
dream of (doing) something* · · · · · · · ·	think about something that you want to happen in the future
drop by* ·	make a short visit
throw cold water on something · · · · · ·	discourage a plan, an idea, a dream, etc.
go by* ·	pass
now and then · · · · · · · · · · · · · · · · · ·	sometimes
go back (to a place)* · · · · · · · · · · · · ·	return (to a place)
be capable of doing something · · · · · ·	have the ability to do something
make an A (a B, etc.) · · · · · · · · · · · · ·	earn a grade (*A, B*, etc.) in school
hit the books · · · · · · · · · · · · · · · · · · ·	study

recycled idioms: grow up, give up   *phrasal verb (see Lexicon and Appendix D)

86 Can You Believe It?   *Book 2*

2. Listen

Cover the story and look only at these pictures. Listen to the story two or three times.

3. Read the Story

Now read the story carefully. Pay special attention to the idioms so that you're ready for Exercise 4.

4. Listen and Complete

Close your book. Listen to the story again. When the tape or your teacher pauses, try to complete the idiom.

5. Tell the Story

Cover the story and look at the pictures above. Tell the story using as many idioms as you can.
a. First, work with the whole class to retell the story.
b. Then tell the story to a partner or small group.

6. Answer the Questions

About the story . . . .

a. What kind of child was Torres?

b. What did he dream of doing?

c. What happened when Torres spoke to his counselor?

d. As the years went by, what did Torres talk about?

e. Why did his first college professor change his life?

f. What is the moral of this story? Do you know people like the high school counselor and the college professor?

About you . . . .

g. Tell about a dream you had that came true.

h. Are you a bookworm?

i. For how long do you hit the books on a typical evening?

j. What do you dream of doing in the future? Does your family encourage you to follow your dreams, or do they throw cold water on them?

7. Write About Yourself

a. I often drop by _____ in order to _____.

b. Someday I want to go back to _____ because _____.

c. I dream of _____ and _____ in the future.

d. Now and then, I _____.

8. Write a Poem

Write a poem about your dreams for the future using at least three idioms from the unit.

9. Take a Dictation

_____

_____

_____

_____

_____

10. Complete the Dialogue

a. Read this true story and fill in the blanks with idioms from the box.

> • went by
> • a bookworm
> • came true
> • made an A
> • go back
> • dream of

Great-great Grandmother Graduates

San Juan, Puerto Rico At the age of 102, Ana Molina made an unusual decision. She decided to (1)_____ to high school.

Eighty-six years ago, Molina had to leave school. Her family had no money, and she needed to work. Many years (2)_____, but she continued to (3)_____ getting her high school diploma.

Eight months after going back to school, Molina's dream (4)_____. She graduated from high school. A native speaker of Spanish, Molina is very proud that she (5)_____ in English.

Molina is a poet and (6)_____. She reads literature to the children in her poor neighborhood. "I'm in love with life," says the great-great grandmother.

recycled idiom: be in love with

b. Read or tell the story to a partner.

Bullfighting Is in Her Blood

20

1. Quick Reading

Look at the pictures on page 91.
What is the story about?

Now read quickly to get the main idea.

SPAIN ¹When Cristina Sanchez was a little girl, she loved to watch her father fight bulls. ²She knew that bullfighting was a dangerous profession. And she knew that there were no women bullfighters in Spain. ³But still she wanted to become a matador, to follow in her father's footsteps. So at the age of 12, Cristina started practicing with cows.

⁴Her father **was** totally **opposed to** her future plans. "It's impossible. Women don't become bullfighters," he said. But Cristina insisted. "I didn't want the role of a traditional woman," she says. ⁵Finally, her father **changed his mind** and **gave in**. He saw that Cristina had bullfighting **in her blood**. He **gave her the green light** to attend the most famous school in Spain to **learn the ropes** of bullfighting. And then he became her trainer.

⁶Now Cristina is a star in her country. As the first female matador, she is always **in the public eye**. ⁷But it hasn't been **smooth sailing** for her. She has been hurt three times by bulls. ⁸Also, many people **are angry about** her participation in the sport. Some male matadors refuse to share the bullring with her, and she often hears insults from the audience. "When I hear insults from the crowd," says Cristina, "it makes me try harder. I want those people to **eat their words**."

New idioms and expressions

in one's blood ·	in one's personality or character
be opposed to something · · · · · · · · · · · · ·	disagree strongly with a plan, an idea, etc.
change one's mind · · · · · · · · · · · · · · · · · · ·	begin to think differently about something
give in* ·	agree to something you didn't want to agree to before
give someone the green light · · · · · · · · ·	give someone permission to do or start something
learn the ropes ·	learn how to do something
in the public eye · · · · · · · · · · · · · · · · · · ·	well known; in the news
smooth sailing ·	easy and without problems
be/get angry about something · · · · · · · ·	feel very upset or unhappy about a situation
eat one's words ·	admit that what one said is wrong

recycled idiom: follow in someone's footsteps   *phrasal verb (see Lexicon and Appendix D)

2. Listen

Cover the story and look only at these pictures. Listen to the story two or three times.

3. Read the Story

Now read the story carefully. Pay special attention to the idioms so that you're ready for Exercise 4.

4. Listen and Complete

Close your book. Listen to the story again. When the tape or your teacher pauses, try to complete the idiom.

5. Tell the Story

Cover the story and look at the pictures above. Tell the story using as many idioms as you can.
a. First, work with the whole class to retell the story.
b. Then tell the story to a partner or small group.

6. Answer the Questions

a. How did Cristina's father first feel about her plans for the future?

b. Why did he finally change his mind?

c. Where did Cristina learn the ropes of bullfighting?

d. Why hasn't it been smooth sailing for Cristina?

e. What do you think of the matadors who refuse to share the bullring with Christina? Do you know men like this?

f. What do you think of Cristina's career choice? What do you think about the sport of bullfighting?

About you..

g. Is your family opposed to any of your ideas or dreams?

h. Tell about a time when you were opposed to something but then gave in.

i. From what you see on TV and read in the newspapers, who is in the public eye now? What do you know about these people?

7. Write about Yourself

Complete the sentences, writing something true about yourself.

a. I'm angry about _____.

b. I'm opposed to _____

    because _____.

c. In my country, _____ is in the public

    eye because _____.

8. Write a Dialogue

Work with a partner. Write a dialogue using at least three idioms from the unit. Act it out for a small group or the class.

9. Take a Dictation

_____

_____

_____

_____

_____

10. Complete the Dialogue

a. A mother and her teenage son, Kenny, are talking. Fill in the blanks with idioms from the box.

> • **give in**
> • **be angry about**
> • **give me the green light**
> • **learn the ropes**
> • **opposed to**
> • **change my mind**

Hi, honey. How was your first day at work?

It wasn't bad. I'm starting to (1)_____. In a few months, I'll have enough money for a motorcycle.

You know I don't like motorcycles. I'm absolutely (2)_____ the idea.

But Stefano has one. And a lot of other kids do too.

I know, but I think motorcycles are very dangerous.

But, Mom, …

I'm not going to (3)_____. You won't make me (4)_____.

Oh, Mom. **Have a heart!*** You have to (5)_____ on this one!

Sorry, Kenny. Please don't (6)_____ this. It's for your own good.

*Have a heart!: Be kind and nice!

b. Work with a partner. Role-play the dialogue together.

A. Parts of the body: Many idioms use parts of the body. Complete these idioms. Then match them to their meanings.

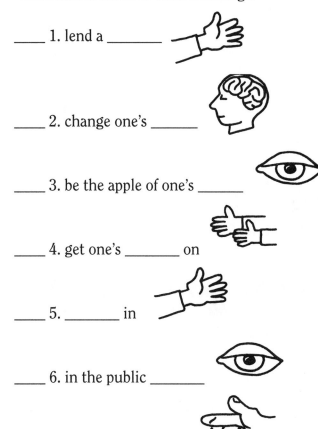

_____ 1. lend a _____

_____ 2. change one's _____

_____ 3. be the apple of one's _____

_____ 4. get one's _____ on

_____ 5. _____ in

_____ 6. in the public _____

_____ 7. in one's _____

a. give something that is due to someone

b. help

c. get ahold of

d. well known; in the news

e. be one's favorite person or thing

f. in one's personality or character

g. change one's opinion on an issue

B. Odd one out: Cross out the word or phrase that doesn't go with the verb.

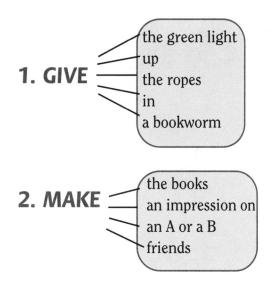

1. GIVE
- the green light
- up
- the ropes
- in
- a bookworm

2. MAKE
- the books
- an impression on
- an A or a B
- friends

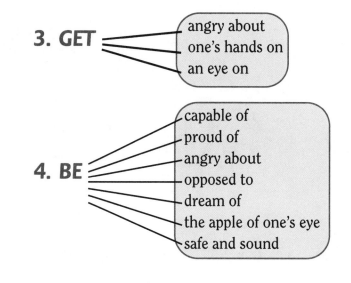

3. GET
- angry about
- one's hands on
- an eye on

4. BE
- capable of
- proud of
- angry about
- opposed to
- dream of
- the apple of one's eye
- safe and sound

C. When, Where, or How? Do these expressions answer the question *When?*, *Where?*, or *How?* Write the expressions under the correct question word.

now and then   **on time**   **knocked out cold**
behind bars   **cool as a cucumber**   **scared out of one's wits**
in the public eye   **in the end**   **in one's blood**
safe and sound   **all over the place**   **on the spot** *(use two times)*

When?	Where?	How?

D. Of, in, on, or out? Complete the expressions with the correct words. Use each word four times.

1. be capable _____
2. throw cold water _____
3. knocked _____ cold
4. find _____
5. _____ the end
6. _____ the public eye

7. be proud _____
8. _____ the spot
9. _____ time
10. dream _____
11. get one's hands _____

12. Look _____!
13. give _____
14. _____ one's blood
15. get out _____
16. roll _____ the red carpet

E. Good or bad? Is the speaker feeling good or bad? Write the sentences in the correct box.

I'm scared out of my wits.   **It has been smooth sailing.**
I'm proud of what I've done.   **I'm angry about it.**
I'm safe and sound.   **She's throwing cold water on my dreams.**
I'm having the time of my life.   **I'm going to be put behind bars.**
My dreams are coming true.   **I made an *A*!**
I've turned over a new leaf.   **They're rolling out the red carpet for me.**

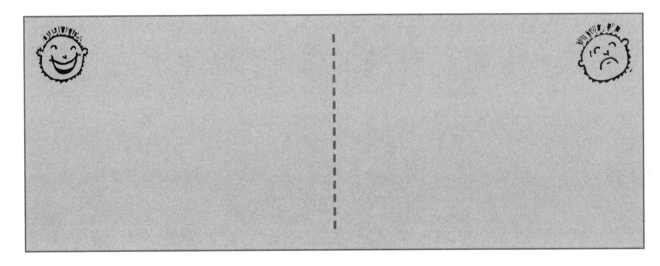

F. Idioms in pictures: What idioms do these pictures illustrate? Complete the idioms.
Then match them to their meanings. Draw lines.

A

B

1. eat one's _____

a. in prison

2. give the _____

b. behave better

3. be a _____

c. one's favorite person or thing

4. behind _____

d. greet someone with hospitality

5. turn over a new _____

e. admit what you said isn't correct

6. throw cold _____ on
something

f. discourage someone's plans

7. the _____ of one's eye

g. give the OK to start something

8. roll out the red _____

h. learn how to do something

9. smooth _____

i. love reading

10. learn the _____

j. easy and problem-free

G. Find someone who... Fill in the chart below with names of classmates. Try to write a different name in each blank. Stand up and walk around the classroom. Ask questions such as:

Do you want to be in the public eye?
Do you have music in your blood?

Find someone who...

1. ...wants to be in the public eye.	
2. ...has music in his/her blood.	
3. ...is always on time.	
4. ...is proud of his/her English.	
5. ...is going to take a trip soon.	
6. ...is a bookworm.	
7. ...dreams of becoming a movie star.	
8. ...made an A in class recently.	
9. ...wants to make more friends.	
10. ...is opposed to the sale of guns.	
11. ...often gets angry.	
12. ...wants to turn over a new leaf.	
13. ...dreams of taking a trip to Japan.	
14. ...is capable of speaking three languages.	

Appendix A: Answer Key

1. It's No Wonder!
page 5: 1. has a stomachache, 2. is running a fever, 3. right away, 4. get rid of, 5. It's no wonder, 6. made the mistake

2. It's About Time!
page 9: 1. get married, 2. it's about time, 3. tie the knot, 4. I'm in seventh heaven, 5. can afford, 6. cost an arm and a leg

3. A Heart of Gold
page 13: 1. grew up, 2. is used to, 3. was sick, 4. has a heart of gold, 5. gave away, 6. are getting in touch with

4. Fit as a Fiddle
page 17: 1. senior citizen, 2. out of shape, 3. work out, 4. fit as a fiddle, 5. in shape, 6. feel like a million dollars, 7. not believe her eyes

5. Longest Hair in the World
page 21: 1. give you a hand, 2. come in handy, 3. In fact, 4. take care of, 5. according to, 6. take ages

Review: Units 1-5
page 22:   A. 1. heart (e), 2. feet (b), 3. eyes (d), 4. an arm and a leg (a), 5. hand (c)
B. 1. the knot, 2. a mistake, 3. sick, 4. in handy, 5. a blue moon

page 23:   C. 1. in, 2. in, 3. in, 4. out, 5. in, 6. in, 7. out, 8. on, 9. in, 10. out, 11. in
D. GOOD: I'm fit as a fiddle., I'm in seventh heaven., I'm in shape., I'm healthy., I feel like a million dollars., I'm in love.
BAD: I'm out of shape., I made a mistake., I'm running a fever., I have a stomachache.
E. 1. c, 2. e, 3. d, 4. c, 5. b, ages, right away, day in and day out, once in a blue moon, at long last

page 24:   F. Answers may vary.
G. 1. d, 2. f, 3. a, 4. e, 5. b, 6. c

page 25: H. Answers will vary.

6. Lost Skier Dances All Night Long
page 29: 1. are looking for, 2. keeps her head, 3. by herself, 4. in the nick of time, 5. is frozen stiff, 6. all right, 7. give up

7. Spaniards Paint the Town Red
page 33: 1. paint the town red, 2. once a year, 3. I'm getting ready, 4. throw a party, 5. I'm dying to, 6. go bananas

8. Man Dances at His Own Funeral
page 37: 1. look like a million bucks, 2. ripped off, 3. I'm feeling blue, 4. get over, 5. dumbfounded, 6. go crazy

9. Fish Turns the Tables on Fisherman

page 41: 1. in hot water, 2. crazy about, 3. show off, 4. take it easy, 5. play it safe, 6. let go

10. The Ringing Dog

page 45: 1. what is going on, 2. looking high and low, 3. vanish into thin air, 4. figure out,
     5. a little bit later, 6. get the picture

Review: Units 6–10

page 46:   A. 1. be on cloud nine, 2. go bananas, 3. sleep like a log, 4. be in hot water,
     5. be on top of the world

     B. 1. easy, 2. on cloud nine, 3. into thin air, 4. mistake, 5. ready

page 47:   C. 1. in, 2. on, 3. off, 4. in, 5. on, 6. on, 7. off, 8. on, 9. off, 10. in

     D. GOOD: I'm on cloud nine., I'm taking it easy., I look like a million dollars., I'm having a great
     time., I'm crazy about this food., I'm on top of the world.
     BAD: I'm in hot water, I'm frozen stiff, I'm scared to death, I'm really getting lost, I feel blue,

     E. 1. b/f, 2. b/f, 3. d, 4. e, 5. a, 6. c, Once a year, all night long, All at once, Before long/A bit later,
     Before long/A bit later, in the nick of time

page 48:   F.

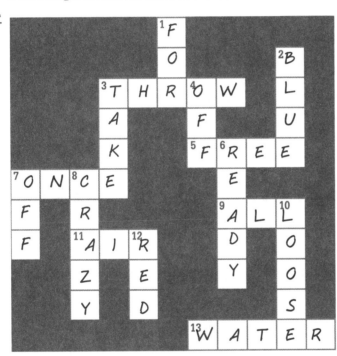

     G: 1. c, 2. d, 3. e, 4. a, 5. b

page 49:   H. Answers will vary.

11. Robber Chickens Out

page 53: 1. at last, 2. chicken out, 3. run away, 4. take a look at, 5. make sense of, 6. spend time

12. Lovesick Elephant

page 57: 1. passed away, 2. brokenhearted, 3. look after, 4. going from bad to worse, 5. cheer me up,
     6. fall head over heels in love

13. Shoplifter Gets a Dose of His Own Medicine

page 61: 1. give me a lift, 2. just in time, 3. raining cats and dogs, 4. a while, 5. in a hurry, 6. I'm hungry

14. Crow Commits Crime

page 65: 1. made off with, 2. for good, 3. was in a bad mood, 4. pulled into, 5. caught his eye, 6. wide-eyed

15. On the Cutting Edge

page 69: 1. the icing on the cake, 2. Spend time on, 3. Go shopping, 4. Try out, 5. I'm interested in

Review: Units 11–15

page 70:   A. 1. tooth (c), 2. heart (a), 3. head, heels (e), 4. handed (f), 5. eye (b), 6. eyed (d)

B. Be: hungry, interested in, on the cutting edge, (sure), brokenhearted, in a hurry
Go: shopping, from bad to worse, (off with)
Make: money, sense of, sure, off with

page 71:   C. 1. up, out, away, 2. up, away, 3. on, out

D. Confusion or surprise: can't make heads or tails of, wide-eyed, What in the world?, can't make sense of
Fear: chicken out, run away, lose one's nerve
Sadness or depression: die of a broken heart, be in a bad mood, be brokenhearted

E. 1. over and over, 2. just in time, 3. for good, 4. after a while, 5. all of a sudden, 6. at last

page 72:   F. 1. dogs (b), 2. cake (g), 3. footsteps (f), 4. time (a), 5. medicine (d), 6. money (c), 7. sight (e)

G. 1. The robber tried to hold the bank up. The robber tried to hold it up.
2. Frank Landstrom was happy to get his gold bracelet back. Frank Landstrom was happy to get it back.
3. At REI, you can try hiking boots on. At REI, you can try them on.
4. You can also try boots out on the test trail. You can also try them out on the test trail.

Page 73: H. Answers will vary.

16. Man Tries to Turn Over a New Leaf

page 77:   1. on the spot, 2. first-rate, 3. am signing up for, 4. it turns out that, 5. as well as, 6. on time, 7. turn over a new leaf

17. Gorilla Lends a Helping Hand

page 81: 1. the apple of her eye, 2. Look out, 3. lend him a hand, 4. scared out of his wits, 5. safe and sound

18. Money Rains from the Sky

page 85: 1. took a trip, 2. had the time of my life, 3. all over the place, 4. rolled out the red carpet, 5. found out, 6. made a big impression on

19. Janitor's Dream Comes True

page 89: 1. go back, 2. went by, 3. dream of, 4. came true, 5. made an A, 6. a bookworm

20. Bullfighting Is In Her Blood

page 93: 1. learn the ropes, 2. opposed to, 3. give in/change my mind, 4. give in/change my mind, 5. give me the green light, 6. be angry about

Review: Units 16–20

page 94:   A. a. hand (b), 2. mind (g), 3. eye (e), 4. hands (c), 5. eye (d), 6. blood (f)
B. 1. the ropes, 2. the books, 3. an eye on, 4. dream of

page 95:   C. When?: now and then, in the end, on the spot
          Where?: behind bars, in the public eye, all over the place, in one's blood, on the spot
          How?: safe and sound, on time, cool as a cucumber, knocked out cold, scared out of one's wits

   D. 1. of, 2. on, 3. out, 4. out, 5. in, 6. in, 7. of, 8. on, 9. on, 10. of, 11. on, 12. out, 13. in, 14. in, 15. of, 16. out

   E. GOOD: I'm proud of what I've won; I'm safe and sound; I'm having the time of my life; My dreams are coming true; I've turned over a new leaf; It has been smooth sailing; I made an A!; They are rolling out the red carpet for me
      BAD: I have to face the music now, I'm scared out of my wits, I'm angry about it, She is throwing cold water on my dreams, I'm going to be put behind bars

page 96: F. 1. words (e), 2. green light (g), 3. bookworm (i), 4. bars (a), 5. leaf (b), 6. water (f), 7. apple (c), 8. carpet (d), 9. sailing (j), 10. ropes (h)

page 97: G. Answers will vary.

Appendix B: Dictations

1. It's No Wonder!
Olga **has a stomachache**. She's also **running a fever**. So she goes to see her doctor. He takes an X-ray. He sees a medical instrument inside Olga. "**No wonder!**" he thinks. He wants to **get rid of** it **right away**. But Olga wants to **put off** the operation. She **has cold feet**. Maybe she is afraid that the doctors will **make a mistake** again!

2. It's About Time!
Sebastio **is in love.** He asks Vittoria to marry him. Vittoria wants to **get married**, too. But she **can't afford** the wedding dress she wants. So she asks Sebastio to wait and he agrees. He waits and waits. Vittoria saves up for 40 years. **At long last**, Vittoria has her dress and she's ready to **tie the knot. It's about time!**

3. A Heart of Gold
When Victor Bacelis **picks up** the money, he is surprised. He **gets in touch with** police and gives the money to them. But they **give it back**. Then Victor decides to **give it away** to a little boy who **is sick**. "I'm healthy. I have enough money," he says. This man **has a heart of gold**.

4. Fit as a Fiddle
Ed was **out of shape** when he was 84. Then he started to **work out**. He **pumped iron day in and day out**. Now, at age 91, he **feels like a million dollars**. He's **as fit as a fiddle**. His family and friends **cannot believe their eyes**!

5. Longest Hair in the World
Hoo's hair is hard to **take care of**. He washes it **once in a blue moon**. It **takes ages** to dry. But he says it **comes in handy** in cold weather. **And according to** Hoo, when people **get sick**, he can help them.

6. Lost Skier Dances All Night Long
Karen Hartley is skiing **by herself** and **gets lost**. She **is scared to death**, but she **keeps her head.** She dances **all night long** to stay warm. She doesn't **give up**. The next morning, a helicopter comes for her **in the nick of time**. She is cold but **all right**.

7. Spaniards Paint the Town Red
Bunyol **throws a** tomato **party once a year**. The town **gets ready** by putting plastic over the windows. When the tomatoes arrive, the party begins. People throw tomatoes at each other. They really **let loose**. They **go bananas**. Everyone **has a great time.**

8. Man Dances at His Own Funeral
Ahmed's friends are **feeling blue**. They think he died. When they see him walk in, they **are dumbfounded**. He **looks like a million dollars**! Ahmed explains that a thief **ripped** him **off** and took his ID cards. The funeral **turns into** a party. Everyone **is on top of the world**!

9. Fish Turns the Tables on Fisherman
A Russian man is **showing off** for his friends. He kisses a fish on the mouth. But the fish **turns the tables on** the man. It bites his nose and won't **let go**. His friends **cut** the head **off** the fish, but it still won't **let go**. Finally, a doctor **sets** the man **free**.

10. The Ringing Dog

When the phone disappears, Rachel can't **figure** it **out**. She **looks high and low for** it. She suspects the dog, who is **sleeping like a log**. Finally, she dials the number. She hears ringing in the dog's stomach. "**What in the world?**" she thinks. **All at once**, she **gets the picture**.

11. Robber Chickens Out

A robber was trying to **hold up** a bank. He gave a note to the teller, but she **couldn't make heads or tails** of it. Several clerks **took a look at** the note. They couldn't **make sense of** it either. Finally, the robber **lost his nerve** and **ran away**.

12. Lovesick Elephant

Pankov **was brokenhearted** when Mako **passed away**. Mako **looked after** her for 34 years. Zookeepers could not **cheer** her **up**. **Over and over** they tried to feed her, but she refused all food. She **went from bad to worse**. On Valentine's Day, Pankov **died of a broken heart**.

13. Shoplifter Gets a Dose of His Own Medicine

A man saw Tear Drop on the road and **gave him a lift**. It was **raining cats and dogs**. **After a while**, the man **was hungry** and stopped at a supermarket. He tried to **shoplift**, but the store manager **caught him red-handed**. When the man walked out of the store, he saw Tear Drop **taking off** with his truck. The man **got a dose of his own medicine**.

14. Crow Commits Crime

A crow came **out of nowhere** and **made off with** Frank's bracelet. Frank was certain the bracelet was gone **for good**, and he **was in a bad mood**. But later, a man found the bracelet 35 miles away. Then he saw a story about Frank in the paper. He **put two and two together** and gave the bracelet back to Frank.

15. On the Cutting Edge

People like to **go shopping** at REI. Shoppers can **try out** boots on a hiking trail. If they **are interested in** buying a bike, they can **try** one **out** on a bike trail. The hands-on store is **making** a lot of **money**. REI **is on the cutting edge**. Experts say more stores will **follow in its footsteps**.

16. Man Tries to Turn Over a New Leaf

Michael Backman tried to **turn over a new leaf**. When he returned to Grant High School, he **made friends** right away. He was a **first-rate** student and **handed in** his homework **on time**. But he couldn't hide from the police. He is now **behind bars** for his new crime **as well as** his old ones.

17. Gorilla Lends a Helping Hand

One day, a small boy at a zoo climbed over a wall into the gorilla habitat. He fell 24 feet and **was knocked out cold**. His mother **was scared out of her wits**. But Binti-Jua was **as cool as a cucumber**. She **kept** the other gorillas **away**. The boy is now **safe and sound**. The zoo director **is proud of** the gorilla. She **is the apple of his eye**.

18. Money Rains from the Sky

When a truck crashed, money from the truck flew **all over the place**. Many people ran to **get their hands on** it. Police told people to return the money, but **in the end**, only two people **showed up**. Because Herbert gave back the money, DisneyWorld invited his class to **take a trip** there. They **rolled out the red carpet** for the children.

19. Janitor's Dream Comes True

As a boy, Primo Torres **was** a **bookworm**. He **dreamed of** becoming a teacher, but his counselor **threw cold water on** his dream. So Torres got a job as a janitor at Mayfield High School. The years **went by**. When he was 41, Torres **went back** to school. Now Torres is teaching at Mayfield High School. His dream has **come true**.

20. Bullfighting Is in Her Blood

Cristina grew up with bullfighting **in her blood.** Her father **was opposed to** her plans at first. But finally he **gave in.** He **gave her the green light** to study bullfighting. She attended school in Spain to **learn the ropes.** Now she is a star in Spain, always **in the public eye.**

Appendix C: Idiom groups

This appendix categorizes idioms and expressions in different ways to help you learn and remember.

p. 108–110 *Idioms grouped according to form*

p. 108   Idioms that use:
Food
Colors
Numbers
Music
Temperature
Body Parts
Animals
The Skies

p. 109   Idioms that use:
Time
Questions
And
Like
As

p. 110   Idioms that use verbs:
Get
Make
Keep
Take
Go
Give
Put
Turn
Look
Have

pp. 111–113 *Idioms grouped according to meaning*

p. 111   Idioms related to feelings

p. 112   Idioms related to changes

p. 113   Idioms related to health, money, and time

Idioms grouped according to form

Food
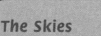
That takes the cake!
(as) flat as a pancake
go bananas
the icing on the cake
(as) cool as a cucumber
be the apple of one's eye

The Skies
be in seventh heaven
be on top of the world
be on cloud nine
once in a blue moon
vanish into thin air

Animals

chicken out
rain cats and dogs
be a bookworm

Body Parts
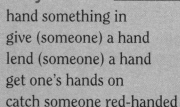
hand something in
give (someone) a hand
lend (someone) a hand
get one's hands on
catch someone red-handed

not believe one's eyes
be the apple of one's eye
catch one's eye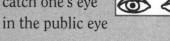
in the public eye

keep one's head
fall head over heels
in love
change one's mind

have a heart of gold
be brokenhearted
die of a broken heart

have a sweet tooth
have cold feet
cost an arm and a leg
at the top of one's lungs
lose one's nerve
in one's blood

Idioms that use...

Colors
once in a blue moon
paint the town red
feel blue
catch someone red-handed
roll out the red carpet
give (someone) the green light

Numbers
first-rate
love at first sight
all at once
put two and two together
be in seventh heaven
be on cloud nine
feel like a million dollars
look like a million dollars

Temperature
be in hot water
have cold feet
be frozen stiff
be knocked out cold
as cool as a cucumber
throw cold water on

Idioms grouped according to form

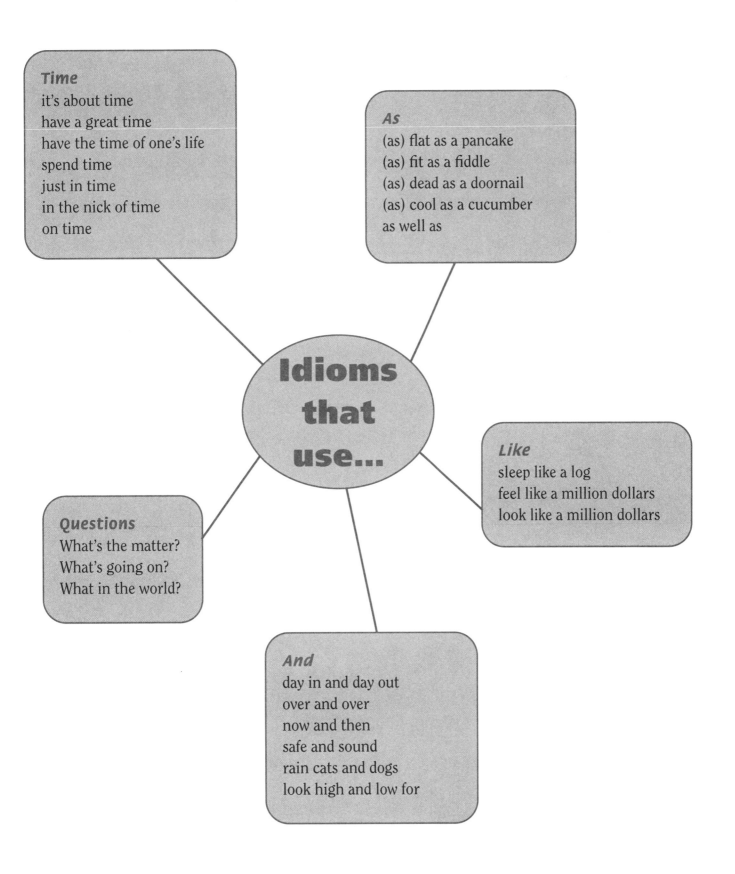

Time
it's about time
have a great time
have the time of one's life
spend time
just in time
in the nick of time
on time

As
(as) flat as a pancake
(as) fit as a fiddle
(as) dead as a doornail
(as) cool as a cucumber
as well as

Idioms that use...

Like
sleep like a log
feel like a million dollars
look like a million dollars

Questions
What's the matter?
What's going on?
What in the world?

And
day in and day out
over and over
now and then
safe and sound
rain cats and dogs
look high and low for

Idioms grouped according to form

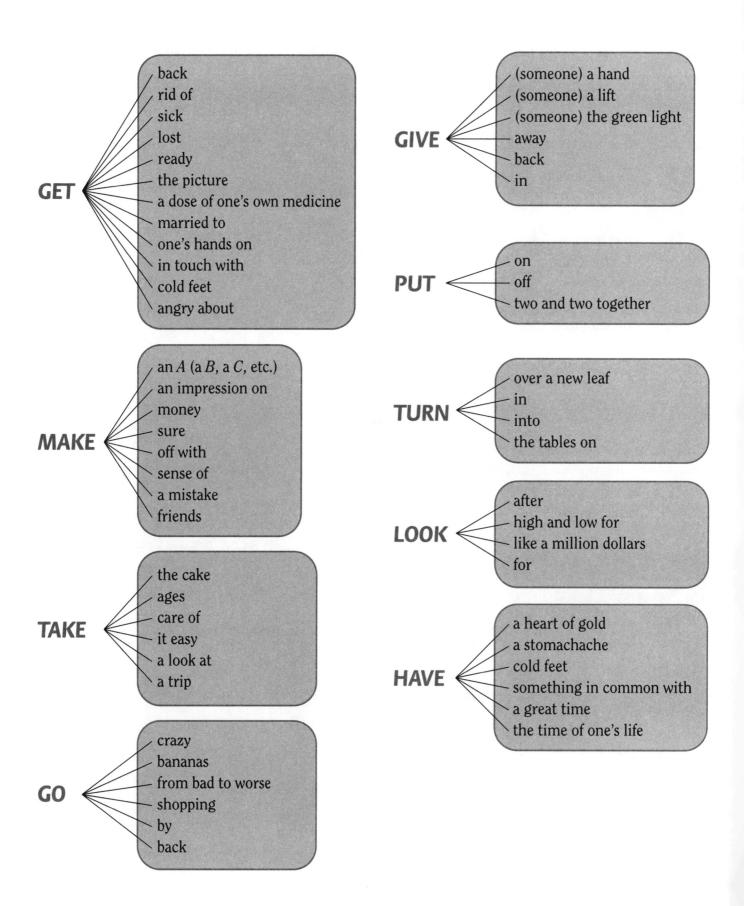

GET
- back
- rid of
- sick
- lost
- ready
- the picture
- a dose of one's own medicine
- married to
- one's hands on
- in touch with
- cold feet
- angry about

MAKE
- an *A* (a *B*, a *C*, etc.)
- an impression on
- money
- sure
- off with
- sense of
- a mistake
- friends

TAKE
- the cake
- ages
- care of
- it easy
- a look at
- a trip

GO
- crazy
- bananas
- from bad to worse
- shopping
- by
- back

GIVE
- (someone) a hand
- (someone) a lift
- (someone) the green light
- away
- back
- in

PUT
- on
- off
- two and two together

TURN
- over a new leaf
- in
- into
- the tables on

LOOK
- after
- high and low for
- like a million dollars
- for

HAVE
- a heart of gold
- a stomachache
- cold feet
- something in common with
- a great time
- the time of one's life

Idioms grouped according to meaning

Feelings

Happy
be in seventh heaven =
be on cloud nine =
be on top of the world

feel like a million dollars
be in a good mood
be in love
be proud of
have a great time
have the time of one's life
fall head over heels in love

Unhappy
feel blue
be in a bad mood

be in hot water
be brokenhearted

Physically comfortable
(as) fit as a fiddle
in shape
all right
be healthy
safe and sound

Physically uncomfortable
be frozen stiff
be/get sick
out of shape
be hungry
run a fever
have a stomachache

Confused/Surprised/Angry
be wide-eyed
be dumbfounded
be/get lost
be/get angry about

Calm
(as) cool as a cucumber
take it easy
keep one's head

Enthusiastic
be dying to
be crazy about
be interested in

let loose
go bananas
go crazy

Afraid
be scared out of one's wits
be scared to death

Idioms grouped according to meaning

Changes

Change in size, shape, or intensity

grow up
cut off
vanish into thin air
get in shape
die down

Change in health status

get sick   die of a broken heart
go from bad to worse   pass away

Change in marital status

tie the knot
get married

Change in feeling, attitude, or habit

fall in love
fall head over heels in love
get over
get cold feet, chicken out, lose one's nerve
turn over a new leaf
turn the tables on someone
cheer up
give in
eat one's words

Change in understanding/clarity

get the picture=make sense of=put two and two together=figure out
get lost

General change in the situation

turn into   go by
come true   go back
it turns out that

Idioms grouped according to meaning

Health

+	–
be healthy	be sick
(as) fit as a fiddle	get sick
in shape	out of shape
feel like a million dollars	run a fever
look like a million dollars	knocked out cold
be all right	go from bad to worse
safe and sound	(as) dead as a doornail
pump iron	pass away
work out	die of a broken heart

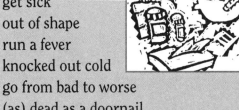

Money

make money
can afford
cost an arm and a leg
save up
give away

Crimes involving money
rip off
hold up

Time

How often?	*Regularly:*	day in and day out
	Sometimes:	now and then; once a year
	Rarely:	once in a blue moon
	Immediately:	right away; on the spot
	After a short time:	before long; a little bit later
	After a long time:	at last; at long last; it's about time; in the end
	Continually:	all night (day, week, month, year) long
	Repeatedly:	over and over
	Suddenly:	all of a sudden; all at once
	Forever:	for good
	A long time:	ages
	In time:	just in time; in the nick of time

Appendix D: Phrasal Verbs

I. What is a phrasal verb?

A phrasal verb is a verb + a particle.

> *Sylvain goes to the gym twice a week to **work out.***
> (verb)(particle)
>
> *The woman **gave** 1 million dollars **away.***
> (verb)   (particle)

In English, many phrasal verbs are idiomatic; you can't understand the meaning of the whole from the parts. *Work out* means "exercise", and *give away* means "give something as a gift."

II. Phrasal verbs fall into different categories.

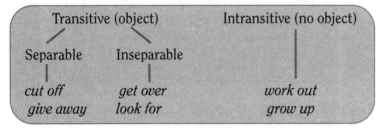

a. Some phrasal verbs are *transitive;* others are *intransitive.*

Transitive phrasal verbs take a direct object.

> *I **cut off** <u>my</u> hair.*
> *He **gave away** <u>his old bike</u>.*

Intransitive phrasal verbs do not take an object.

> *I like to **work out**.*
> *Jaime is really **growing up**.*

b. Some transitive phrasal verbs are *separable* (that is, the object can come between the two parts of the verb); others are *inseparable.*

Separable phrasal verbs	Inseparable phrasal verbs
cut off	**get over**
*I **cut off** my hair.*	*She can't **get over** her cold.*
*I **cut** my hair **off**.*	*She can't **get over** it.*
*I **cut** it **off**.*	
give away	**look for**
*He **gave away** his bike.*	*I'm **looking for** my cat.*
*He **gave** his bike **away**.*	*I'm **looking for** it.*
*He **gave** it **away**.*	

When a phrasal verb is *separable,* you can put a noun between the verb and the particle or after the particle. If you use a pronoun (*he, she, it, we, you, they*), the pronoun must go between the verb and particle. If a phrasal verb is *inseparable,* the noun and pronoun always come after the particle.

III. Phrasal verbs from this book

CHEER UP (transitive, inseparable): make someone happier
*The movie was funny, and it **cheered up** Bob.*
*The movie was funny, and it **cheered** Bob **up**.*
*The movie was funny, and it **cheered** him **up**.*

CHICKEN OUT (intransitive): decide not to do something you planned because you're afraid
*I would like to try river rafting, but I always **chicken out**.*

CUT OFF (transitive, separable): remove something (often with a knife or scissors)
*She **cut off** the tree branches.*
*She **cut** the tree branches **off**.*
*She **cut** them **off**.*

DIE DOWN (intransitive): come slowly to an end; grow weaker
*The storm was very heavy an hour ago, but now it has **died down**.*

DREAM OF (transitive, inseparable): think about something that you would like to happen
*Daisy **dreams of** being a movie star.*
*Daisy **dreams of** it.*

DROP BY (transitive, inseparable): make a short visit
*Let's **drop by** the library this evening.*
*Let's **drop by** it this evening.*

FIGURE OUT (transitive, separable): solve a problem; understand something
*Can you **figure out** this math problem?*
*Can you **figure** this math problem **out**?*
*Can you **figure** it **out**?*

FIND OUT (transitive, usually inseparable); learn; discover something
*Did you **find out** their plan?*
*Did you **find** it **out**?* Note: This verb is only separable when "it" is used.

GET BACK (transitive, separable): receive something that belonged to you before
*I **got back** my car from the repair shop.*
*I **got** my car **back** from the repair shop.*
*I **got** it **back** from the repair shop.*

GET OVER (transitive, inseparable): recover from a physical illness or emotional shock
*I hope you **get over** the flu soon.*
*I hope you **get over** it soon.*

GET RID OF (transitive, inseparable): remove something
*Will you please **get rid of** this junk?*
*Will you please **get rid of** it?*

GIVE AWAY (transitive, separable): give something as a gift
*I'm going to **give away** my bicycle; I don't ride it anymore.*
*I'm going to **give** my bicycle **away**; I don't ride it anymore.*
*I'm going to **give** it **away**; I don't ride it anymore.*

GIVE BACK (transitive, separable): return something (to someone)
*Please **give back** my pencil.*
*Please **give** my pencil **back**.*
*Please **give** it **back**.*

GIVE IN (intransitive): agree to something you didn't want to agree to before
*Lonnie wants me to change my mind, but I will never **give in**.*

GIVE UP (intransitive): stop trying; quit
*Learning to dance isn't easy for him, but he never **gives up**.*

GO BACK (intransitive): return to a place
*I have to **go back** to the library tomorrow to return a book.*

GO BY (intransitive): pass
*I saw the bus **go by**.*

GROW UP (intransitive): become an adult
*Billy is really a big boy; he is **growing up**.*

HAND IN (transitive, separable): give something that is due to someone
*Please **hand in** your tests now.*
*Please **hand** your tests **in** now.*
*Please **hand** them **in** know.*

HOLD UP (transitive, separable): rob someone or something at gunpoint
*The thief **held up** the tourists and took their money.*
*The thief **held** the tourists **up** and took their money.*
*The thief **held** them **up** and took their money.*

KEEP AWAY (transitive, separable): make (someone or something) stay at a distance
*Please **keep away** that dog.*
*Please **keep** that dog **away**.*
*Please **keep** it **away**.*

KEEP ON (transitive, inseparable): continue doing something
*He wants to **keep on** studying English.*
*He wants to **keep on** studying it.*

LET GO OF (transitive, inseparable): stop holding; release
*Please **let go of** my arm.*
*Please **let go of** it.*

LOOK AFTER (transitive, inseparable): take care of
*Will you **look after** my house while I'm gone?*
*Will you **look after** it while I'm gone?*

LOOK FOR (transitive, inseparable): try to find someone or something
*She's **looking for** her glasses.*
*She's **looking for** them.*

LOOK OUT! (intransitive): Be careful!; Be alert!
***Look out!** The pan is very hot.*

MAKE OFF WITH (transitive, inseparable): take or steal something
*The shoplifter **made off with** a leather jacket.*
*The shoplifter **made off with** it.*

PASS AWAY (intransitive): die
*Ten year ago, my grandmother **passed away**.*

PICK UP (transitive, separable): take or lift something off the floor (or a table, etc.)
*I cleaned my room and **picked up** my clothes.*
*I cleaned my room and **picked** my clothes **up**.*
*I cleaned my room and **picked** them **up**.*

PULL INTO (transitive, inseparable): drive one's car into a place
*The driver **pulled into** the parking lot.*
*The driver **pulled into** it.*

PUT OFF (transitive, separable): delay or postpone something
*We're going to **put off** our trip for two months.*
*We're going to **put** our trip **off** for two months*
*We're going to **put** it **off** for two months.*

PUT ON (transitive, separable): dress in something; place something on oneself
*It's cold; you should **put on** a sweater.*
*It's cold; you should **put** a sweater **on**.*
*It's cold; you should **put** it **on**.*

RIP OFF (transitive, separable): steal from someone; steal something
*The thief **ripped off** my car.*
*The thief **ripped** my car **off**.*
*The thief **ripped** it **off**.*

RUN AWAY (intransitive): leave quickly; escape
*Jane's dog **ran away**.*

SAVE UP (transitive, separable): keep money so one can use it later
*I'm going to **save up** my money to buy a car.*
*I'm going to **save** my money **up** to buy a car.*
*I'm going to **save** (it)**up** to buy a car.* (Note: the reference to money can be omitted with this verb, but it is an implied object)

SIGN UP FOR (tansitive, inseparable): agree to do something by writing your name
*I **signed up for** a Chinese class yesterday*
*I **signed up for** it yesterday*

SHOW OFF (intransitive): try to attract attention to oneself
*John is always **showing off**.*

SHOW UP (intransitive): arrive; appear
*The party starts at 9:00 PM. What time will you **show up**?*

SIGN UP FOR (transitive; inseparable): agree to do something by writing your name
*I **signed up for** a Chinese class yesterday.*
*I **signed up for** it yesterday.*

TAKE CARE OF (transitive, inseparable): provide for the needs of
*She likes to **take care of** her garden.*
*She likes to **take care of** it.*

TAKE OFF (intransitive): leave a place (by car, on foot, or by plane)
*The plane **took off** at 12:30.*

TRY ON (transitive, separable): test the fit of shoes or clothes
*Why don't you **try on** those jeans?*
*Why don't you **try** those jeans **on**?*
*Why don't you **try** them **on**?*

TRY OUT (transitive, separable): test something to see if it works
*You should **try out** the bike before you buy it.*
*You should **try** the bike **out** before you buy it.*
*You should **try** it **out** before you buy it.*

TURN IN (transitive, separable): give something to someone
*Please **turn in** your exams now.*
*Please **turn** your exams **in** now.*
*Please **turn** them **in** now.*

TURN INTO (transitive, inseparable): become something different
*A caterpillar **turns into** a butterfly..*
*A caterpillar **turns into** it.*

WORK OUT (intransitive): exercise
*We like to go to the gym to **work out**.*

LEXICON

Idiom and Definition	Usage	Example	Language notes	Similar expressions	Opposite expressions
a little bit later (10) a short time later		I'm busy with a customer now. Can I call you a little bit later?		a little later a bit later in a little while in a bit (informal)	
according to someone or something (5) as someone or something says		According to the weather report, it's not going to rain today.	*According to* is not followed by *me*. Instead, use *in my opinion.*	in the words of	
after a while (13) later; a short time later	informal	Murat can't talk to you now, but he'll be free after a while. Can he call you back?		in a while later on	right away (= immediately)
all at once (10, 17) suddenly; unexpectedly		I was sitting quietly when all at once the room started shaking. It was an earthquake!	*All at once* also means all *at the same time*, as in *The students tried to speak all at once.*	all of a sudden	
all night long (6) during the entire night		I couldn't sleep last night. I was awake all night long.		all week long all month long all year long	
all of a sudden (8, 14, 16) suddenly; unexpectedly		I was sleeping when all of a sudden a loud noise woke me up.		all at once	
all over the place (18) everywhere		This park has garbage and litter all over the place; we need to clean it up.		here, there, and everywhere (informal) all over creation (slang)	in one spot

Idiom and Definition	Usage	Example	Language notes	Similar expressions	Opposite expressions
all right (6) fine; OK		Jane feels all right today. All right, children, you can have some ice cream.	In informal English, *all right* has the same uses as *OK*. The expression can also mean *Hooray!* or *Wonderful!*	A-OK (slang)	so-so
(as) cool as a cucumber (17) very calm and relaxed	informal	Ali was cool as a cucumber during the emergency. He helped everyone escape.	The first *as* can be omitted. The expression usually occurs with the verb *be*.	have nerves like steel (informal)	be on edge be a bundle of nerves (informal) be a nervous wreck (informal)
(as) dead as a doornail (8) completely dead	informal	No wonder this radio doesn't work! The batteries are as dead as a doornail.	The first *as* can be omitted. The expression usually occurs with the verb *be*.	(as) dead as a dodo	
(as) fit as a fiddle (4) healthy and physically fit	informal	Chin swims and runs every day and is as fit as a fiddle.	The first *as* can be omitted. The expression usually occurs with the verb *be*.	in great shape	out of shape as sick as a dog (informal)
(as) flat as a pancake (4) very flat	informal	I can't drive my car. One tire is flat as a pancake.	The first *as* can be omitted. The expression usually occurs with the verb *be*.		
as well as (16) and also; in addition to		I enjoy tennis as well as soccer.	As well as is used in the middle of a sentence to connect two things. *As well* is used at the end of a sentence: *I enjoy tennis and soccer as well.*	in addition to	

LEXICON

A B C D E F G H I J K L M N O P Q R S T U V W X Y Z

Idiom and Definition	Usage	Example	Language notes	Similar expressions	Opposite expressions
at last (11) finally; after a long time		I waited a long time for the bus. When it arrived at last, it was full!		at long last	right away
at long last (2) after a very long time; finally		Dolly has been working on her PhD. for ten years; at long last, she's finished!		at last	right away
at the top of one's lungs (7) very loudly		It was impossible to sleep because the children were shouting at the top of their lungs.	Common verbs occurring before this expression are *talk*, *yell*, and *shout*.	at the top of one's voice	in a whisper in a low voice under one's breath
be a bookworm (19) love to read		Bobby is a bookworm. He never turns on the TV; he prefers to read.		always have one's nose in a book (informal) be crazy about books/reading (informal)	
be/get angry about something (20) feel very upset or unhappy about a situation		Anna was angry about losing her job.	The expression is followed by a noun or a gerund. You can also be angry *at* someone or *with* someone.	be/get mad about (informal) see red lose one's temper hit the ceiling (slang) have a fit (informal) blow up about something (informal) be/get hot under the collar about something (informal) be (as) mad as a hornet (informal) be (as) mad as hell (informal)	keep calm keep one's temper

Idiom and Definition	Usage	Example	Language notes	Similar expressions	Opposite expressions
be brokenhearted (12) be very sad		I was brokenhearted when I heard that my best friend had died.	Other expressions based on *break* and *heart* are *break someone's heart, die of a broken heart,* and *be heartbroken.*	be heartbroken have a heavy heart	be on cloud nine be in seventh heaven be on top of the world
be capable of doing something (19) have the ability to do something		Mimosa has had a lot of work experience, so we're sure she's capable of managing that company.			be incapable of doing something be hopeless at doing something
be crazy about someone or something (9) like someone or something very much	informal	I'm crazy about mambo dancing. Do you like it?	Use a noun or gerund after the expression.	be mad/nuts/wild about something or someone (informal) be hooked on something (informal)	be lukewarm about something (informal) can't stand someone or something (informal)
be dumbfounded (8) be unable to speak because of shock or surprise		I was dumbfounded when I heard that Paul and Stella were moving to Florida.		be at a loss (for words) lose one's tongue	
be dying to do something (7) want to do something very much	informal	I'm dying to see my family; I've been away from them so long!	Don't confuse this expression with *be dying of. I'm dying of thirst* means *I'm very thirsty.*	be eager to do something be itching to do something (informal)	be half-hearted about doing something be unenthusiastic about doing something
be frozen stiff (6) be very cold		Juanita walked home in the snow without a hat or gloves; she was frozen stiff.	This expression is used only with people, not things.	be chilled to the bone	be as warm as toast (informal) be thawed out

LEXICON

A B C D E F G H I J K L M N O P Q R S T U V W X Y Z

Idiom and Definition	Usage	Example	Language notes	Similar expressions	Opposite expressions
be healthy (3) be well; have good health		Liliana had cancer a few years ago, but now she's healthy.		be in the pink (informal) be healthy as a horse (informal, = very healthy) be fit as a fiddle (informal)	be unhealthy be sick be under the weather (informal, = be sick)
be hungry (13) have an appetite; want to eat		The children are hungry, so let's stop for lunch now.		be as hungry as a horse/bear (informal, = be very hungry) be starving (slang, = very hungry)	be full be stuffed (slang)
be in a bad mood (14) feel angry or sad		Makiko is in a bad mood today because she lost her wallet.		be in bad spirits be out of sorts (informal) be in bad sorts (informal)	be in a good mood be in good spirits
be in hot water (9) be in a difficult situation; be in trouble	informal	We'll be in hot water if our car runs out of gas.	The expression is also used with *get into* as in *She got into hot water.* It can be followed by *with*, as in *I'm in hot water with my boss.*	in a bind/jam/fix/ tight spot/ pickle (informal) be in trouble be up the creek (informal)	get out of a jam get out of trouble get out of a mess
be in love (with someone) (2) love (someone) strongly in a romantic way		Yoshi seems so happy. Maybe he's in love. But who could he be in love with?		fall in love with someone or something	fall out of love with someone

120 Can You Believe It?   *Book 2*

Idiom and Definition	Usage	Example	Language notes	Similar expressions	Opposite expressions
be interested in something (15) want to do or have something		Jorge is interested in starting his own business.	This expression is followed by a noun or gerund.	be into something (slang) be hot on something (informal)	be uninterested in (doing) something be half-hearted about (doing) something
be in seventh heaven (2) be very happy	informal	I'll be in seventh heaven if I get the new job.		be on cloud nine (informal) be on top of the world (informal) be walking on air (informal)	be down in the dumps (informal) be down at the mouth (informal) be/feel blue
be knocked out cold (17) become unconscious from a blow to the head		The man was hit by a golf ball and was knocked out cold.		be out cold be out like a light (informal)	come to (= regain consciousness)
be on cloud nine (9) be very happy	informal	Ly was on cloud nine when he won the lottery.		be on top of the world (informal) be in seventh heaven (informal) be walking on air (informal)	be down in the dumps (informal) be down at the mouth (informal) be/feel blue
be on the cutting edge (of something) (15) be the leader (in a certain field)		That computer software company is on the cutting edge of the industry.		be in the vanguard be ahead of one's time blaze a trail set the pace lead the pack (informal)	be outdated be behind the times
be on top of the world (8) feel very happy	informal	Monika will be on top of the world if she wins the scholarship.		be sitting on top of the world (informal) be walking on air (informal) be in seventh heaven (informal) be on cloud nine (informal)	be down in the dumps (informal) be down at the mouth (informal) be/feel blue

Idiom and Definition	Usage	Example	Language notes	Similar expressions	Opposite expressions
be opposed to something (20) disagree strongly with a plan, an idea, etc.		Ruben is opposed to the project, and he refuses to support it financially.	The expression can also be followed by a gerund, as in *He's opposed to smoking* or *I'm opposed to your going to New York.*	be against something be dead set against something (= be very opposed to something) turn thumbs down on something	be in favor of (doing) something be behind (a plan, an idea, etc.) turn thumbs up on something
be proud of someone or something (17) be very pleased with someone or something		He's proud of his daughter; she just graduated from medical school.	Reflexive pronouns are used with this expression, as in *I'm proud of myself.* It can also be followed by a gerund, as in *I'm proud of my singing.*	be (as) proud as a peacock of someone or something (informal, = be very proud of)	be ashamed of someone or something
be scared out of one's wits (17) be very afraid	informal	They were scared out of their wits when the man pulled out a gun.		be scared to death (informal) be frightened to death (informal) be scared stiff (slang) be petrified (slang)	be (as) cool as a cucumber (informal)
be scared to death (6) feel very afraid	informal	The mother was scared to death when she couldn't find her child.	The phrase *to death* can also be used informally to mean *very* in the following phrases: *frightened to death, bored to death, thrilled to death.*	be frightened to death (informal) be scared out of one's wits (informal) be scared stiff (slang)	be (as) cool as a cucumber (informal)

Idiom and Definition	Usage	Example	Language notes	Similar expressions	Opposite expressions
be sick (3) be unwell; have bad health		She's sick today and won't be going to school.	Note that *I'm going to be sick* means *I'm going to vomit.*	be under the weather (informal) be sick as a dog (informal, = be very sick) be on one's last legs/have one foot in the grave (slang, = be close to death)	be healthy feel like a million dollars
be the apple of one's eye (17) be one's favorite person or thing		Ly is the apple of his grandmother's eye. She gives him whatever he wants.		have a soft spot in one's heart for someone	be the bane of one's existence be an albatross around one's neck
be used to (doing) something (3) be familiar with (doing) something		I'm used to eight hours of sleep a night. I'm used to sleeping eight hours a night.		*Be used to* is always followed by a noun or a gerund. It refers to a habit that continues in the present. Don't confuse it with *used to*, which indicates a past situation or habit and is followed by the base form of the verb as in *I used to live in Mexico.*	be accustomed to (doing something) be in the habit of (doing something)

Idiom and Definition	Usage	Example	Language notes	Similar expressions	Opposite expressions
before long (7) soon		Mother Earth will be destroyed before long if we don't take care of the environment.		in a little while (informal)	
behind bars (16) in prison		They put the criminal behind bars for 20 years.		in the slammer (slang) in the joint (slang)	on the loose at large
by mistake (6) accidentally; because of a mistake		Here's your book, Eva. I took it home yesterday by mistake.		in error	on purpose by choice
by oneself (6) alone		I offered to go with Alida, but she wanted to take the trip by herself.		on one's own all alone all by oneself	in a group in concert with someone accompanied by someone
can afford something (2) have enough money to buy something		I can afford to take a few days off from work, but I can't afford to go anywhere! I'll just stay home.	The expression can be followed by a noun *(I can afford that car)* or an infinitive *(I can't afford to rent that apartment).*		
cannot make heads or tails of something (11) not able to understand something	informal	I have to reread this chapter. I read it once, but I couldn't make heads or tails of it.		it's Greek to me can't make sense of something	make sense of something figure something out get it (informal)

Idiom and Definition	Usage	Example	Language notes	Similar expressions	Opposite expressions
catch one's eye (14) attract one's attention		The dress in the window caught Maria's eye, so she went in and bought it.		catch one's attention attract one's attention	
catch someone red-handed (13) catch someone who is committing a crime		Two people tried to break into my car, but a security guard caught them red-handed.		catch someone in the act	
change one's mind (20) begin to think differently about something		I was going to buy a car, but I changed my mind. I bought a motorcycle instead.	Plural: *They changed their minds. We changed our minds.*		make up one's mind (= decide definitely)
cheer someone up (12) make someone happier		I tried to cheer Susan up by telling some funny stories. I tried to cheer up Susan by telling some funny stories.	Phrasal verb (trans, sep) This expression also means *become happy.* Used in this way, it is intransitive (*Please cheer up!*).		make someone miserable
chicken out (11) not do something you planned because you're afraid	informal	I was going to go rock climbing, but I chickened out. It's too dangerous.	Phrasal verb (intrans) *Chicken out of* is transitive, as in *I chickened out of skiing.*	get cold feet be a chicken (informal)	pluck up one's courage have the nerve to do something (informal) get up the nerve to do something (informal)
come in handy (5) be useful or convenient	informal	Be sure to take mosquito spray on your camping trip. It will come in handy!		be useful be convenient	serve no purpose be useless

Idiom and Definition	Usage	Example	Language notes	Similar expressions	Opposite expressions
come true (19) become real; change from dream to fact		Nina thinks her dreams of becoming an actress will come true when she moves to Hollywood.			
cost an arm and a leg (2) be very expensive	informal	My new car cost an arm and a leg. My bank account is empty now.	You can also *pay an arm and a leg* for something.	cost a fortune (informal) cost a pretty penny (informal)	be dirt cheap (informal) cost peanuts (informal)
cut something off (9) remove something (often with a knife or scissors)		I cut the legs off my jeans and made shorts. I cut off the legs of my jeans and made shorts.	Phrasal verb (trans, sep)		
day in and day out (4) regularly; all the time		Stefano loves pasta and eats it day in and day out.	Also written and spoken as *day in, day out*.	day after day week in and week out year in and year out	now and then (= occasionally)
die down (18) come slowly to an end; grow weaker		The wind was very strong this morning, but it has died down.	Phrasal verb (intrans) *Die down* is used only for things (fire, wind, excitement, etc.), not for people.	die away fizzle out peter out	flare up
die of a broken heart (12) die from sadness		After his wife's death, the old man was very unhappy. Before long, he died of a broken heart.			
dream of (doing) something (19) think about something that you want to happen in the future		Jose loves airplanes and dreams of becoming a pilot someday.	Phrasal verb (trans, insep) *Dream of* is followed by a noun or a gerund.		

Idiom and Definition	Usage	Example	Language notes	Similar expressions	Opposite expressions
drop by (19) make a short visit		Why don't you drop by tonight?	Phrasal verb (intrans or trans, and insep) You can *drop by* a place (*Let's drop by the library*). When you talk about a person, use the possessive (*Let's drop by Jim's house*).	drop in stop by drop into	
eat one's words (20) admit that what one said is wrong	informal	Marco told me I would not succeed; now he has to eat his words.		eat crow (informal) eat humble pie (informal) back down	
excuse oneself (11) ask permission to leave a person or place		The meeting went on for more than two hours. Finally, I excused myself and left.	The expression can also mean *ask to be excused for doing something that is impolite. (John excused himself for not remembering my name).*		
fall head over heels in love (with someone) (12) fall deeply and suddenly in love		Bashkim fell head over heels in love with Natasha and asked her to marry him two weeks after they met.	You can also *be head over heels in love.*	fall for someone (informal) fall in love with someone	fall out of love with someone
feel blue (8) be sad		I always feel blue when it rains day after day.	You can also *be blue.*	be down in the dumps (informal) be down at the mouth (informal)	be on cloud nine (informal) be in seventh heaven (informal) be on top of the world (informal) feel like a million dollars (informal)

Idiom and Definition	Usage	Example	Language notes	Similar expressions	Opposite expressions
feel like a million dollars (4) be very healthy and happy		I slept really well last night! I feel like a million dollars this morning.	*Bucks* can be used instead of *dollars* as in *I feel like a million bucks*. These words (*bucks/dollars*) can also be omitted: *I feel like a million.*	look like a million (dollars/bucks)	feel like death warmed over feel like something the cat dragged in
figure something out (10, 11) solve a problem; understand something		Tony can't figure out the math problem. Tony can't figure the math problem out.	Phrasal verb (trans, sep) Don't confuse *figure out* with *find out*, which means *learn or discover.*	put two and two together make sense of something catch on to something	be in the dark can't make heads or tails of something (informal)
find something out (18) learn; discover something		I want to find out the truth. I want to find it out.	Phrasal verb (trans, usually insep) Separable only when a pronoun is used, as in the second example.		
first-rate (16) excellent		The food at the new Japanese restaurant is first-rate.	This is an adjective.	top-drawer (informal) top-notch (informal)	third- rate
follow in someone's footsteps (15, 20) follow someone's example		Esmeralda decided to follow in her father's footsteps and became a teacher, too.		follow in someone's tracks	

Idiom and Definition	Usage	Example	Language notes	Similar expressions	Opposite expressions
for good (14, 16) forever; permanently		Mitsu likes his job in Tokyo. He plans to stay there for good.	This phrase is often used in the expression *gone for good.*		for a little while for a time for the time being for the moment
get a dose of one's own medicine (13) get the same bad treatment you give other people	informal	Leonid always refuses to help his coworkers. Now he's getting a dose of his own medicine because they have refused to help him on his new project.	You can also *give others a dose of their own medicine* or *have a dose of your own medicine.*	get a taste of one's own medicine	
get something back (14) receive something that belonged to you before		I got back my books from George. I got my books back from George.	Phrasal verb (trans, sep)		give back
get in touch with someone (3, 14) contact someone by phone, fax, e-mail, etc.		I'll get in touch with Alex to see if he can come to the meeting.		touch base with someone (informal) be in touch with someone, keep/ stay in touch with someone get back in touch with someone	be out of touch with someone lose touch with someone
get lost (6) become unable to find one's way (home)		It's hard to get lost in New York City because most of the streets are numbered and laid out in a grid pattern.	*Get lost!* is slang for *Go away!*		find one's way
get married (to someone) (2) marry (someone)		Did you know that Lola got married to my cousin?	After you *get married,* you *are married.*	tie the knot (with someone) (informal)	get a divorce (from someone) get divorced (from someone) split up (with someone) (informal)

LEXICON

Idiom and Definition	Usage	Example	Language notes	Similar expressions	Opposite expressions
get one's hands on something (18) take ahold of something	informal	I've been looking for this book for a long time. I finally got my hands on it!		lay one's hands on something	let go of something
get over something (8) recover from a physical illness or an emotional shock		I'm shocked by John's behavior. I can't get over it. I can't get over this cold.	Phrasal verb (trans, insep)		
get ready (7) prepare		I have to get ready to take the TOEFL exam. I have to get ready for work now.	*get ready + to do something* *get ready + for something*	get (all) set (to do something) get (all) set (for something)	
get rid of something (1) remove something		I cleaned my closet and got rid of all my old clothes.	Phrasal verb (trans, insep) Sometimes *be* is used in this expression: *I'd like to be rid of that old car.*	throw something away	hang on to/hold on to something (= keep something)
get sick (5) become unwell or unhealthy		I got sick right before the trip, so I had to stay home in bed.		come down with something catch a bug (informal) catch a cold get the flu	get better get well get over (a cold, the flu, an illness)
get the picture (10) understand the situation or the facts	informal	At first, I didn't see why Alida was so unhappy with her new job; then I met her boss and now I get the picture.		get it (informal) figure (something) out	be in the dark be clueless (slang)

Idiom and Definition	Usage	Example	Language notes	Similar expressions	Opposite expressions
give something away (3) give something as a gift		When he got his new computer, he gave away his old one. When he got his new computer, he gave his old one away.	Phrasal verb (trans, sep)		
give something back (3, 18) return something (to someone)		Can you give back my dictionary? I need it. Can you give my dictionary back? I need it.	Phrasal verb (trans, sep)		get back
give in (20) agree to something you didn't want to agree to before		Melissa refused to sign the contract at first, but finally she gave in and signed it.	Phrasal verb (intrans) *Give in to* is a transitive phrasal verb, as in *She gave in to her son and let him have the car.*	back down cave in	hold one's ground stand one's ground
give someone a hand (5) help someone		That suitcase looks heavy. Can I give you a hand?	You give someone a hand *with* something (*I'll give you a hand with the dishes.*) *Give someone a hand* also means *applaud.*	lend someone a (helping) hand help someone out	not lift a finger/hand to help someone
give someone a lift (13) give someone a ride in your car or truck		Jorge gave me a lift home because I missed the bus.	You can also *ask someone for a lift* or *get a lift from someone.*	give someone a ride pick someone up	
give someone the green light (20) give someone permission to do or start something		My boss gave me the green light to buy new office furniture.	The expression is also used with *get*, as in *I got the green light to buy new office furniture.*	give someone the go-ahead	stand in someone's way be opposed to something

Idiom and Definition	Usage	Example	Language notes	Similar expressions	Opposite expressions
give something up (6, 19) stop trying; quit something		Don't give up! If you keep trying, you'll be successful.	Phrasal verb (intrans) *Note that give up (doing) something (trans) means stop doing something, as in He gave up cigarettes and wants to give up drinking too.*	throw in the towel (slang)	keep on trying
go back (to a place) (19) return (to a place)		I went to Chicago last week, but I have to go back there again next month.			
go bananas (7) become very excited and act wildly		The fans went bananas when their team won the soccer game.		go nuts/crazy/out of one's mind (informal) lose it (slang) flip out (slang)	keep one's cool (informal) not bat an eyelid (informal)
go by (19) pass		Time goes by so fast.	Phrasal verb (intrans) Note that *go by* can also be transitive as in *I go by the park on my way to school.*		
go crazy (8) become very excited and act wildly		The man went crazy when he heard he won the lottery.		go bananas/nuts out of one's mind (informal) lose it (slang) flip out (slang)	keep one's cool (informal) not bat an eyelid (informal)
go from bad to worse (12) go from a bad situation to a very bad situation		Our trip went from bad to worse. We missed the plane, and then we all got sick.		go downhill	take a turn for the better get better

Idiom and Definition	Usage	Example	Language notes	Similar expressions	Opposite expressions
go shopping (15) shop		Boris likes to go shopping at Bell's Department Store because they have all the latest Italian fashions.			
grow up (3, 19) become an adult		She grew up in Zaire, but left after high school to attend college in the United States.	Phrasal verb (intrans)	be born and raised (in a place)	
hand something in (16) give something that is due to someone		Please hand in your keys before you leave. Please hand your keys in when you leave.	Phrasal verb (trans, sep)	turn something in	hand something back
have a great time (7) enjoy oneself very much		We had a great time at the beach yesterday.	*Good, wonderful, super, nice,* or *fabulous,* are often used instead of *great* in this expression.	have a good time have a super time (informal) have a ball (slang)	have a horrible/rotten/ miserable/lousy time (informal)
have a heart of gold (3) have a kind and generous character		Sofia helps me whenever she can; she really has a heart of gold.		be bighearted	have a heart of stone
have a stomachache (1) feel pain in one's stomach		I have a stomachache. I think the chicken I ate was bad.	The verb *have* is used in many expressions for illness: *have a fever, have an earache, have a headache, have the flu, have a cold,* etc.		

Idiom and Definition	Usage	Example	Language notes	Similar expressions	Opposite expressions
have a sweet tooth (12) love to eat sweet foods		Raoul loves to eat cakes, pies, and cookies; he really has a sweet tooth!		be a sugar freak (slang) be a chocoholic	can't stand sweets
have cold feet (1) be afraid to do something		I always have cold feet when I speak in front of a large audience.	Also used with *get,* as in *John got cold feet and decided not to go.*	be chicken (informal)	have the nerve to do something (informal)
have something in common with someone (5) be like another person in some way		Sally and her brother have something in common. They're both musicians and great cooks.	*A lot, much, a few things, a great deal, etc.,* can be used instead of *something* as in *I have a lot in common with my mother.*	be two peas in a pod (informal, = have a lot in common)	have nothing in common (with someone) be as different as night and day (informal)
have the time of one's life (18) have a wonderful time		We took the children to the zoo, and they had the time of their lives.		have a good time have a great time	have a horrible time (informal)
hit the books (19) study	informal	Eduardo is a good student. He hits the books four or five hours a night.	This expression is often used with *have to,* as in *I can't go out tonight. I have to hit the books.*		not crack a book (informal, = not open a book, not study)
hold someone or something up (11) rob someone or something at gunpoint		Two teenagers held up the woman and took all her money. Two teenagers held the woman up and took all her money.	Phrasal verb (trans, sep) This expression has several other meanings as well, including *delay, hold high,* and *last/endure.*		

Idiom and Definition	Usage	Example	Language notes	Similar expressions	Opposite expressions
in a hurry (13) rushed; need to move quickly		I'm in a hurry this morning because I have to catch the early train to work.	This expression is often followed by an infinitive as in *I'm in a hurry to leave.*	in a rush pressed for time	in no hurry take one's time (= verb phrase)
in fact (5) really; actually		She has an amazing gift for languages; in fact, I think she speaks five or six.	This expresssion is often used to emphasize or restate what has just been said.	in point of fact as a matter of fact	
in one's blood (20) in one's personality or character		Tara's very good at acting; it's in her blood. Both her parents are actors.		in the blood in one's genes	
in shape (4) in good physical condition		My doctor told me to get in shape by swimming every day.	This expression is commonly used with the verbs *be, get, keep,* and *stay.*	in condition in good shape as fit as a fiddle (informal)	out of shape
in the end (18) after all; ultimately		She expected to stay in Hong Kong for two weeks, but in the end she stayed only three days.	Don't confuse this expression with *at the end,* which means *at the final part of something,* as in *The movie credits are at the end.*	after all after all was said and done	
in the nick of time (6) at the last possible moment; just before it's too late		I arrived at the airport in the nick of time; the gate was just closing as I boarded.	When you do something *in the nick of time,* you feel relieved and happy that you succeeded.	just in time at the eleventh hour at the last minute just under the wire (informal)	too late
in the public eye (20) well known; in the news		Madonna has been in the public eye for years		in the spotlight in the news in the limelight	out of public view

Idiom and Definition	Usage	Example	Language notes	Similar expressions	Opposite expressions
It's about time (2) It's later than expected!	informal	It's about time! Where were you? I've been waiting a half hour!		it's high time (informal)	it's too late
(it's) no wonder (1) it's not surprising	informal	No wonder the car won't start. The gas gauge is on empty!	Note that *it's* can be dropped in this expression.		
it turns out that (16) what is finally clear is that		It turns out that he is 31 years old.	Another way to say *It turns out that he is 31 years old* is *He turns out to be 31 years old*. You can also say *As it turns out, he is 31 years old.*	it happens that	
(just) in time (13) (just) before the last minute; (just) before the deadline		The report was due on Monday at 12:00 noon. We finished it at 11:50— just in time!		(just) in the nick of time at the eleventh hour at the last minute (just) under the wire (informal)	
keep (someone or something) away (17) make (someone or something) stay at a distance		Keep the baby away from the fire!	Phrasal verb (trans, sep) The object almost always separates *keep* and *away*.		
keep on doing something (6) continue doing something		The teacher told the students to be quiet, but they kept on talking.	Phrasal verb (trans, insep) *Keep on with* is followed by a noun (*I kept on with my work*).	keep right on doing something (*right* adds emphasis)	give up doing something call it quits (informal)
keep one's head (6) stay calm in trouble or danger		Amy kept her head during the emergency; she remained calm and helped people escape.		keep cool keep one's cool (informal)	lose one's head lose it (informal) fall apart push the panic button

Idiom and Definition	Usage	Example	Language notes	Similar expressions	Opposite expressions
learn the ropes (20) learn how to do something	informal	It took Boris about a week to learn the ropes at his new job.	If you *learned the ropes,* you *know the ropes.* You can also *show someone the ropes* so that he or she learns them.	learn the tricks of the trade (informal) learn the ins and outs of something (informal) learn the nuts and bolts of something (informal) learn one's way around something	
lend (someone) a (helping) hand (17) help (someone)		Jack lent me a helping hand with the housecleaning, so it didn't take long.		give someone a hand help (someone) out	not lift a finger to help (someone) not lift a hand to help (someone)
let go (of someone or something) (9) stop holding; release		Children! Don't let go of my hands! Hold my hand. Don't let go!	Phrasal verb (trans, insep) or (intrans) *Let go of* is transitive and inseparable. *Let go* is intransitive.		hold on to someone or something hang on to someone or something
let loose (7) act freely; release energy	informal	Our teacher let loose on the last day of class and started dancing and singing.		blow off steam let off steam let oneself go cut loose	
look after someone or something (12) take care of/ watch over someone or something		The boy's grandmother looks after him while his mother is away.	Phrasal verb (trans, insep)	watch over someone or something care for someone or something	

Idiom and Definition	Usage	Example	Language notes	Similar expressions	Opposite expressions
look for someone or something (6) try to find someone or something		I looked for a birthday gift for my father, but I couldn't find the right thing.	Phrasal verb (trans, insep) An adverb phrase such as *high and low* or *in the kitchen can occur between look* and *for*, but the words cannot be separated by a noun or pronoun.	search for someone or something	
look high and low for someone or something (10) look everywhere for someone or something		She looked high and low for her keys and finally found them in the door.		search high and low for hunt high and low for look all over the place for look in every nook and cranny (informal)	
look like a million dollars (8) look healthy, happy, and attractive	informal	Ana got a new hairdo and lost weight; she looks like a million dollars.	*Bucks* is an informal word for *dollars*, and can be used in very informal situations *(He looks like a million bucks.). Dollars* can be dropped, as in *You look like a million.*	feel like a million dollars	
Look out! (17) Be careful!; Be alert!		Look out! There's a car coming!	Phrasal verb (intrans)	Watch out!	
lose one's nerve (11) become afraid and not do something	informal			chicken out (informal) get cold feet	have the nerve to do something (informal) get up the nerve to do something (informal)

Idiom and Definition	Usage	Example	Language notes	Similar expressions	Opposite expressions
love at first sight (12) love that happens when two people first see each other		When Juan saw Nancy at the party, it was love at first sight. Now they're inseparable.	This is a noun phrase, often used with the verb *be*, as in the example.	fall head over heels in love	
make a mistake (1) do something incorrectly		Doug made a mistake and arrived at the party an hour early.		make an error screw up (slang)	get it right (informal) hit the mark (informal)
make an A (a B, a C, etc.) (19) earn a grade of *A* (*B, C*, etc.) in school		When Billy made an F in his math class, his parents were angry.		get an A (a B, a C, etc.)	
make an impression (on someone) (18) have a memorable effect (on someone)		The film "Titanic" made an impression on people all over the world.	This expression is often used with *big, good, bad, great, terrible,* etc., as in *It made a big impression on me.*		
make friends (16) become friendly with other people		Jose is shy and it's hard for him to make friends.	Note the difference between *I made friends with our neighbor today* and *I made a friend today.*		make enemies
make money (15) make a profit; earn money		Billy needs to make some money this summer before he goes to college.	You can *make big money* or *make good money.*		
make off with something (14) take or steal something		When Lily's roommate moved out of the apartment, she made off with Lily's CDs.	Phrasal verb (trans, insep)	make away with something take something away take off with something	

Idiom and Definition	Usage	Example	Language notes	Similar expressions	Opposite expressions
make sense of something (11) understand something		Can you make sense of this letter?	This expression is often used in the negative with *can't,* as in *I can't make sense of his ideas.*	figure something out	not make heads or tails of something (informal)
make sure (15) check something yourself to be sure about it		Make sure you lock the doors and windows at night because this is a dangerous neighborhood.			
not believe one's eyes (4) not believe what one see's because of surprise or shock	informal	I can't believe my eyes! Your child is completely grown up!	This expression often starts out with *I can't, I couldn't, I don't, I didn't,* and *I could hardly.*	be dumbfounded not believe one's ears (= not believe what you hear because of surprise)	
now and then (19) sometimes		He calls his parents now and then, but I think he should call them more frequently.		every now and then once in a while every so often from time to time off and on on and off	day in and day out on a regular basis
on the spot (16) at that exact time and place	informal	When Drita showed up late for work again, she was fired on the spot.		then and there	
on time (16) at the arranged time; not late		The plane landed on time.	Don't confuse *on time* with *in time,* which means *before the deadline.*	right on time	
once a year (7) one time each year		Susanna takes a vacation only once a year, usually in August.		once a day (= one time a day) once a week (= one time a week) once a month (= one time a month)	

Idiom and Definition	Usage	Example	Language notes	Similar expressions	Opposite expressions
once in a blue moon (5) very rarely	informal	Florida has warm weather the whole year; it only snows there once in a blue moon.			day in and day out on a regular basis
out of nowhere (14) suddenly and unexpectedly		The car came out of nowhere and hit the dog.	This expression is often used with the verbs *come* or *appear*.	out of a clear blue sky out of the blue like a bolt out of the blue	
out of shape (4) not in good physical condition		Spiro is really out of shape; I don't think he'll make the soccer team this year.	This expression commonly occurs with the verbs *be* or *get*.		in shape in good shape in condition as fit as a fiddle (informal)
over and over (12) repeatedly; many times		I don't like that radio station because it plays the same songs over and over.		over and over again again and again time after time time and time again	
paint the town red (7) celebrate wildly	informal	We were out all night, painting the town red. What a great time!		spend a night on the town	
pass away (12) die		Eva took the day off to go to a funeral; her aunt passed away.	Phrasal verb (intrans)	pass on meet one's end kick the bucket (slang)	

Idiom and Definition	Usage	Example	Language notes	Similar expressions	Opposite expressions
pick something up (3, 14, 17) take or lift something off the floor (or a table, etc.)		Children! Pick up your toys! Children! Pick your toys up!	Phrasal verb (trans, sep) *Pick up a room means clean it. Pick up a check means pay the whole bill at a restaurant.*		put something down
play it safe (9) be careful; avoid danger	informal	It's dangerous to walk at night here; let's play it safe and take a taxi.		be careful	play with fire (informal) take a risk run a risk take a chance throw caution to the wind
pull into a place (14) drive one's car into a place		When Yasushi pulled into the driveway, he hit the mailbox.	Phrasal verb (trans, insep) Note that *pull in* is an intransitive verb meaning *arrive,* as in *The train just pulled in.*		pull out of a place
pump iron (4) lift weights	informal	She goes to the gym regularly to pump iron.			
put something off (1) delay or postpone something		I'm putting off my trip until next year. I'm putting my trip off until next year.	Phrasal verb (trans, sep) This expression is followed by a noun as in the example or a gerund *(I put off going to the library until tomorrow).*	put something on hold put something on the back burner (informal) put something on ice (informal)	

Idiom and Definition	Usage	Example	Language notes	Similar expressions	Opposite expressions
put something on (5, 7, 15) dress in something; place something on oneself		Put on your sweater if you're cold. Put your sweater on if you're cold.	Phrasal verb (trans, sep) *Put on* has many other meanings too, such as *pretend, gain weight,* and *produce a performance. Put on a play* means *produce and perform a play.*		take something off
put two and two together (14) figure something out from what one sees, hears, learns, etc.		Kim wasn't home when I got there, but I put two and two together and realized he had gone to a movie.		figure something out see the light catch on to something	be in the dark not make heads or tails of something be at a loss
rain cats and dogs (13) rain very hard	informal	We'll have to forget about the picnic. It's raining cats and dogs.	The expression is usually used in the present continuous.	rain buckets (informal)	
right away (1, 16) immediately		Please come to the table right away! Dinner is ready.		at once right this minute (informal) right off the bat (slang)	after a while in a while later on
rip someone or something off (8) steal from someone; steal something	slang/ informal	Someone ripped off my bag. Someone ripped my bag off. Someone ripped me off.	Phrasal verb (trans, sep) You can *rip off* a person, thing, or place. *The boys ripped off the store* means they stole something from the store.		

LEXICON

A B C D E F G H I J K L M N O P Q **R S** T U V W X Y Z

Idiom and Definition	Usage	Example	Language notes	Similar expressions	Opposite expressions
roll out the red carpet (for someone) (18) welcome an important guest with special treatment		They rolled out the red carpet for the president when he visited their town.	Also, you can *get the red carpet treatment* or *give someone the red carpet treatment*.	put out the welcome mat welcome with open arms	
run a fever (1) have a high body temperature		The baby is running a high fever. Let's call the doctor.	The expression is most often used in the present continuous.	run a temperature have a temperature have a fever	
run away (11) leave quickly; escape		The child ran away when he saw the large dog.	Phrasal verb (intrans) *Run away from* is a transitive phrasal verb (e.g., *The child ran away from the large dog.*)		
safe and sound (17) safe and healthy; with no damage or injury		My parents had to drive 12 hours through the snow and rain, but they arrived here safe and sound.		alive and well all in one piece	in danger
save up (2, 3) keep money so one can use it later		Jemal saved up to buy a new computer.	Phrasal verb (intrans) You can *save up for* something as in the example. *Save up for* is transitive and inseparable, as in *I saved up for a computer.*		

Idiom and Definition	Usage	Example	Language notes	Similar expressions	Opposite expressions
senior citizen (4) a person more than 65 years old		Most of the people at the picnic were senior citizens; Carlos was the only young person.	*Senior citizens* is a polite term for older people; it's more respectful than *old lady, old man,* etc. Senior citizens in the U.S. often receive reduced rates at movie theaters, on airplanes, and so on.		
set someone or something free (9) liberate something or someone		The children caught three butterflies, but then they set them free.			lock someone up put someone behind bars
shoplift (something) (13) steal (something) from a store		The teenagers tried to shoplift, but the hidden camera caught them.	A *shoplifter* is a person who *shoplifts*.	rip something off from a store (slang/informal)	
show off (for someone) (9) try to attract attention to oneself		Look at the way Robert is dancing. He likes to show off!	Phrasal verb (intrans)	blow/toot one's own horn (=brag about one's own accomplishments)	
show up (18) arrive; appear	informal	I invited my friends for dinner at 7:00, but they didn't show up until 8:00.	Phrasal verb (intrans)	turn up	vanish into thin air (=disappear)
sign up for something (16) agree to do something by writing your name		Rika signed up for the dance contest on Saturday.	Phrasal verb *Sign up* is intransitive. *Sign up for* is transitive and inseparable.		cancel out on something

LEXICON

Idiom and Definition	Usage	Example	Language notes	Similar expressions	Opposite expressions
sleep like a log (10) sleep very deeply	informal	I slept like a log last night. I didn't hear the thunderstorm.		sleep the sleep of the dead (informal)	not sleep a wink (informal, = not sleep at all) be wide awake be a light sleeper
smooth sailing (20) easy and without problems	informal	I thought working with so many people would be difficult, but it was smooth sailing all the way.	This expression is used most often with the verb *be*.	clear sailing (informal)	a rough time a hard time heavy/tough going (informal)
spend time doing something (11) use time to do something		I want to spend time working in the garden today.	Phrases such as *a lot of* and *a little* can occur with this expression as in *I spend a lot of time cooking.* Compare the expression with *spend time on*+noun, as in *I spent time on my homework.*		
sure enough (10) as expected	informal	Zoran thought he had done well on the test and, sure enough, he made an A.		sure as shooting (slang)	
take ages (5) take a very long time	informal	It takes ages to send a letter through the mail; why don't you just e-mail me?	*Ages* means *a long time* and also occurs in the following expressions: *for ages, it's been ages, in ages.*	take forever take a coon's age (informal)	take just a moment/minute
take a look at someone or something (11) look at someone or something quickly		Will you take a look at this letter before I send it?		have a look at someone or something	

Idiom and Definition	Usage	Example	Language notes	Similar expressions	Opposite expressions
take a trip (18) travel someplace		I'd like to take a trip this year; I'm tired of staying at home!	*Take* also occurs in the expressions *take a walk, take a hike, take a cruise, take a bus, take a train, etc.*	go on a trip	stay at home
take care of someone or something (5, 17) provide for the needs of someone or something		If you don't take care of those plants, they will die.	Phrasal verb (trans, insep)	look after someone or something care for someone or something	let something go (= not take care of something)
Take it easy! (9) stay calm; relax	informal	Why are you so nervous about that test? Take it easy!	The expression can also be used to mean *goodbye* in informal situations.	Calm down! Hang loose! (informal) Chill out! (slang) Cool it! (slang)	
take off (13) leave a place (by car, on foot, or by plane)	informal	We need to be at school at 12:00, so let's take off at 11:30.	Phrasal verb (intrans) Note that *take something off* means *remove clothing.* This phrasal verb is transitive and separable.		
the icing on the cake (15) the best part		Our vacation was wonderful, but the icing on the cake was the helicopter ride over the Grand Canyon.			
That takes the cake! (1) That's really strange!; That's the worst!	informal	Did you hear that David smashed up Laura's car? That takes the cake, doesn't it?		That beats everything! (informal); That's the limit! (informal)	

Idiom and Definition	Usage	Example	Language notes	Similar expressions	Opposite expressions
throw a party (7) organize and have a party	informal	I'm going to throw a New Year's Eve party. Can you come?	You can *throw a party for* someone, as in *I'm throwing a birthday party for my sister.*	have a party	
throw cold water on something (19) discourage a plan, an idea, a dream, etc.		Elena threw cold water on her husband's plans for a vacation in California because she wanted to go to Mexico.	*Throw* can be replaced by *pour* or *dash* in this expression.	be opposed to something	be behind something
tie the knot (2) marry	informal	Roberto and Berta finally tied the knot after living together for 10 years.	The subject is usually plural (*We tied the knot; they tied the knot.*)	get married get hitched (informal)	get a divorce get divorced split up (informal)
try something on (15) test the fit of shoes or clothes		I tried on lots of shoes before I found a pair I liked. I tried lots of shoes on before I found a pair I liked.	Phrasal verb (trans, sep)		
try something out (15) test something to see how it works		You should always try out a new car before you buy it. You should always try a new car out before you buy it.	Phrasal verb (trans, sep)		
turn something in (18) give something to someone		When do we have to turn in our papers for English class? When do we have to turn our papers in for English class?	Phrasal verb (trans, sep) You can turn in such things as *homework, keys at a hotel,* and *a rental car.*	hand something in	give/hand something back

Idiom and Definition	Usage	Example	Language notes	Similar expressions	Opposite expressions
turn into something (8) become something different		The storm turned into a hurricane.	Phrasal verb (trans, insep)		
turn over a new leaf (16) decide to improve your behavior		On her thirtieth birthday, Diana decided to turn over a new leaf. She stopped smoking, and started working out and eating right.		start over start with a clean slate	
turn the tables on someone (9) change a situation completely so that the unexpected happens		We were losing at the beginning, but then we turned the tables on the other team and won the match.			
vanish into thin air (10) disappear quickly and completely		My keys were on the desk this morning, but they've vanished into thin air!			show up appear out of nowhere (=appear suddenly, without warning)
What in the world? (10, 14) What?; How strange! (an expression of shock or surprise)	informal	What in the world? Why are people screaming and running down the street?	The phrase *in the world* is used to show strong feelings and surprise. It's also used in the expressions *How in the world?, Where in the world?,* and *Why in the world?*	What on earth? (informal) What in the wide world? (informal)	
What's going on? (10) What's happening?	informal	What's going on? Why don't you return my phone calls?	A negative answer to this question is *Nothing (is going on).*	What's up? (informal) What's doing? (informal) What's cooking? (informal)	

LEXICON

Idiom and Definition	Usage	Example	Language notes	Similar expressions	Opposite expressions
What's the matter? (1) What's wrong?		What's the matter with your car? Why doesn't it start?	The expression can be followed by *with*, as in *What's the matter with you?* A negative response is *Nothing (is the matter)*. A different expression, *It doesn't matter*, means *it's not important*.	What's the problem? What's happening?	
wide-eyed (14) very surprised		The child was wide-eyed when she saw snow for the first time.		large-eyed round-eyed	
work out (4) exercise		If I don't work out every day, I start to get fat.	Phrasal verb (intrans) Work something out is a transitive separable verb which has many meanings, including *arrange* (*I worked out a new schedule.*) and *find an answer* (*I worked out the math problem.*).	do one's exercises	